PERFECT LIVES

*Overcoming Nine
Hidden Beliefs That
Stand between You and
a Healthy, Joy-Filled Life*

JENNIFER CROW

**TYNDALE
MOMENTUM**

AN IMPRINT OF TYNDALE HOUSE PUBLISHERS, INC.

Visit Tyndale online at www.tyndale.com.

Visit Tyndale Momentum online at www.tyndalemomentum.com.

TYNDALE is a registered trademark of Tyndale House Publishers, Inc. *Tyndale Momentum* and the Tyndale Momentum logo are trademarks of Tyndale House Publishers, Inc. Tyndale Momentum is an imprint of Tyndale House Publishers, Inc.

Perfect Lies: Overcoming Nine Hidden Beliefs That Stand between You and a Healthy, Joy-Filled Life

Copyright © 2012 by Jennifer Crow. All rights reserved.

Illustration of apple copyright © Natalia Kuzmina/iStockphoto. All rights reserved.

Illustration of ink blot copyright © Pedro Ignácio Loyola Frota/SXC. All rights reserved.

Author photograph taken by Derek Green copyright © 2009. All rights reserved.

Lyrics on pages 27, 39, 49, 75, 95, 111, 127, 145, 171, 191, 211, and 246–247 copyright © Victory Productions, LLC. Used with permission.

Designed by Erik M. Peterson

Published in association with the literary agency of Winters and King, Inc., 2448 E. 81st St., CityPlex Towers, Suite 5900, Tulsa, OK 74137.

Unless otherwise indicated, all Scripture quotations are taken from the *Holy Bible*, New Living Translation, second edition, copyright © 1996, 2004, 2007 by Tyndale House Foundation. (Some quotations may be from the NLT, first edition, copyright © 1996.) Used by permission of Tyndale House Publishers, Inc., Carol Stream, Illinois 60188. All rights reserved.

Scripture quotations marked AMP are taken from the *Amplified Bible*,® copyright © 1954, 1958, 1962, 1964, 1965, 1987 by The Lockman Foundation. Used by permission.

Scripture quotations marked NASB are taken from the New American Standard Bible,® copyright © 1960, 1962, 1963, 1968, 1971, 1972, 1973, 1975, 1977, 1995 by The Lockman Foundation. Used by permission.

Scripture quotations marked NIV are taken from the Holy Bible, *New International Version*,® *NIV*.® Copyright © 1973, 1978, 1984, 2011 by Biblica, Inc.™ (Some quotations may be from the previous NIV edition © 1984.) Used by permission of Zondervan. All rights reserved worldwide. www.zondervan.com.

Scripture quotations marked NKJV are taken from the New King James Version.® Copyright © 1982 by Thomas Nelson, Inc. Used by permission. All rights reserved. *NKJV* is a trademark of Thomas Nelson, Inc.

Scripture quotations marked THE MESSAGE are taken from *The Message* by Eugene H. Peterson, copyright © 1993, 1994, 1995, 1996, 2000, 2001, 2002. Used by permission of NavPress Publishing Group. All rights reserved.

Library of Congress Cataloging-in-Publication Data

Crow, Jennifer.
    Perfect lies : overcoming nine hidden beliefs that stand between you and a healthy, joy-filled life / Jennifer Crow.
        p. cm.
    Includes bibliographical references.
    ISBN 978-1-4143-6734-7 (pbk.)
    1. Christian women—Religious life. 2. Self-esteem in women—Religious aspects—Christianity. 3. Truthfulness and falsehood—Religious aspects—Christianity. 4. Crow, Jennifer. I. Title.
    BV4527.C78 2012
    248.8′43—dc23   2012014953

Printed in the United States of America

18   17   16   15   14   13   12
 7   6   5   4   3   2   1

This book is dedicated to the One who has always given me unconditional acceptance, Maker of heaven and earth, who loves me just as I am.

Contents

Introduction ix

1. Perfect Lies in Action 1
2. Pictures Are Powerful! 27
3. What Is the Truth? 39

The Nine Perfect Lies

4. Perfect Lie Number One: I Am Unlovable 49
   I must meet the standards others have set for me because otherwise I will be unlovable.

5. Perfect Lie Number Two: I Am Worthless 75
   I must prove myself because my worth depends on what I do.

6. Perfect Lie Number Three: I Am Unacceptable 95
   I must gain the acceptance of others because their opinion matters most.

7. Perfect Lie Number Four: I Am Unable 111
   I must pull back because I am less capable than others.

8. Perfect Lie Number Five: I Am a Target 127
   I must protect myself because others are out to get me.

9. Perfect Lie Number Six: I Am Not Angry 145
   I must avoid conflict because expressing my anger is wrong.

10. Perfect Lie Number Seven: I Am Bad 171
    I must be perfect because my actions define who I am.

11. Perfect Lie Number Eight: I Am in Danger 191
    I must always be on guard because trouble is all around me.

12. Perfect Lie Number Nine: I Am Deprived 211
    I must indulge myself in order to be happy.
13. Questions and Answers about Christian Meditative
    Prayer 231

    Acknowledgments 262
    Discussion Guide 265
    Notes 275
    About the Author 277

Introduction

PERHAPS THIS BOOK ISN'T FOR YOU.

Maybe you rarely struggle with feelings of inadequacy, of not measuring up. You may be able to make sense of your life and easily cope with the normal stresses of daily living. You may be able to shake off adversity and find a way to be happy no matter what comes your way. If so, *Perfect Lies* may not have much to offer you.

On the other hand, perhaps you often struggle with feelings of discontentment and discouragement. You may be convinced that if only something good would happen to you—the next great relationship, the promotion at work, the birth of a child—*then* you would be happy. You feel a gnawing hunger in your soul that does not let you enjoy the moments of life as they happen. No matter how perfect your life may seem on the outside, on the inside there is something terribly wrong—and you wonder if you will ever be truly happy.

What accounts for the difference between those who

delight in and those who despair over their lives? I would argue it is not our circumstances. The truth of the matter is, the world in which we live—the world we can see, hear, touch, taste, and feel—is not the only world we experience. Our reality is actually created and orchestrated by our thoughts. Most of us are not even aware of this strange inner world, but the reality we create in our own hearts and minds is fundamentally as real as the air we breathe and the gravity that holds us to this earth. It is a reality that will enslave us—or be the key that will set us free to be the men or women God created us to be.

I did not discover this alternate reality until I found myself in a major health and emotional crisis—one that would either make or break my life. Unfortunately, what I didn't know was killing me. I didn't realize it at the time, but the thoughts and pictures I was constantly creating in my mind were allowing lies to invade and, essentially, destroy my life.

This is the story of how I overcame those lies with the truth—and how you can too.

CHAPTER I

PERFECT LIES IN ACTION

The black, empty suitcase in front of me might as well have been the Grand Canyon. Unfathomable to cross. Impossible to fill.

What was wrong with me?

I sat before my luggage and cried like a baby. It suddenly seemed an insurmountable task to fill the suitcase with necessities for our one-week family vacation to my parents' home in South Texas. My husband, Mark, and I, along with our five children, had made this journey many times throughout the years from our home in Oklahoma City. Why, today, did I feel overwhelmed by the simple task of packing a suitcase?

It was August 4, 2003, and I was at the end of my rope,

completely worn out from battling various illnesses for three years. What had started out as chronic hoarseness in my voice—a seemingly minor problem—had grown into a completely debilitating illness that was sapping away my joy, my energy, my very life.

I was at a breaking point, unable to go on without some kind of breakthrough in my health situation. I needed a change in every area—body, mind, and spirit.

WHERE IT ALL BEGAN

The previous twenty years of my life had certainly been an adventure. I had met my husband, Mark, at the Christian college we both attended. You may not believe in love at first sight, but that's how it happened for us. I was the singer in a student jazz band performing one night in the student union building. Mark was a guest of the audio engineer for our group. The soundman, a mutual friend, introduced us, and within one hour Mark had asked me out on a date. I thought he was so handsome and definitely the coolest guy I had ever dated.

I was kind of a nerdy vocal performance major practicing opera all the time, and suddenly I found myself in love with a fast-talking, outgoing guy who was a great dresser and had dreams for the future. He wanted to go into the ministry, which sounded like an incredibly boring lifestyle to me at the time. I had accepted Christ as a child; I loved and was devoted to God with all my heart, but I had been raised in a traditional denominational church. From my perspective, the life of a minister—and especially his wife—looked very bleak.

Well, I could not have been more wrong, as I soon discovered that life with Mark Crow could never be described as boring. During the first twenty years of our marriage, he served on three different staffs as youth pastor, traveled as an itinerant evangelist, established a pro-life group, and launched and grew a megachurch in Oklahoma City.

During those twenty years, I had done my part to build our marriage, our family, and our life together. We married exactly one week after I graduated from college, and I began working full-time selling and programming computerized phone systems to put Mark through college. After he graduated, I helped him in every endeavor that I could. My music training in college seemed a good fit to help him in his first job as a youth minister. I had been a TV singer on Oral Roberts's weekly television shows and traveled to Hollywood to be a part of the prime-time specials that the university filmed during the early eighties with Barbara Mandrell's producers, Sid and Marty Krofft. Our student group was chosen to sing, dance, and record with Barbara Mandrell, B. J. Thomas, Aretha Franklin, Dale Evans, Stephanie Mills, Teddy Pendergrass, and the Lennon Sisters, among others. With this musical background, I was happy to lead worship, the music ministry, and the youth choir when my husband was a youth pastor at St. Mark's Methodist Church in Victoria, Texas, and then at Victory Christian Center in Tulsa, Oklahoma.

After that, in the course of Mark's time as an itinerant minister, I helped with newsletters and office duties. When he and I started Operation Rescue Tulsa, I was right there with him being arrested for peacefully sitting in front of the doors of abortion clinics to help stop the killing of unborn babies who have no voice to speak on their own behalf. I also followed him in a motor home with our three babies as he literally ran across America from Tulsa to Washington, DC, to bring awareness to the plight of the unborn and the pro-life ministry.

When he felt that he had heard God's direction to plant a church in Oklahoma City, I was a little relieved that at least no traveling or being arrested would be involved! At the time, we had four children under the age of eight, whom I home-schooled. (I homeschooled one or more kids every year for nine years.) When the church launched in 1994, I agreed to be the worship leader until he found someone full-time—ha! Over seventeen years later, I was still overseeing all the worship and media production for our organization . . . but I'm getting ahead of myself.

In 2000, the church was growing rapidly, but I was still the only lead singer at five worship experiences each week, four of them on the weekends. When I first began noticing hoarseness in my voice, therefore, I attributed the problem to vocal fatigue. *Perhaps I'm just oversinging,* I thought. *If I tone it down, maybe the problem will just correct itself.* It didn't.

Ironically, as I was experiencing the first symptoms of what ended up being a serious health crisis, I seemed from the outside to have the perfect life. Our congregation, Victory Church, was one of the largest churches in Oklahoma City, and we had five beautiful children, ages two through fourteen, a wonderful house, and many other blessings that God had provided. I felt extremely fulfilled in my work and ministry as each week I took the microphone in front of thousands of people to sing and lead our congregation in worshiping God through music. You would have thought I should have been the happiest woman alive, but my declining health and the emotions associated with that stress were causing me to feel that virtually every area of my life was falling apart.

Meanwhile, I continued trying to find a solution to the hoarseness. In hopes of relieving what I thought was vocal fatigue, I tried adding in-ear monitors to our sound system so that I could hear my voice better over the loud drums and electronic instruments of our band. That way I would not try to sing so loud at each worship experience. When that didn't help, I investigated the potential of an allergy problem. I had battled congestion for many years—maybe this was the answer I was looking for.

After a year or so of consistent use of prescription allergy drugs, which didn't alleviate my hoarseness, I finally was referred to an ear, nose, and throat doctor who specialized in working with vocalists. That was just the beginning of an endless parade of visits to physicians—and I was beginning to feel like the woman in Mark 5 who had "suffered many things" at the hands of doctors but had nothing to show for it (verse 26, NKJV). I gradually faced a growing awareness that there was a battle raging in my body and my mind. It was a battle not just for my health, but also for my marriage, for my family, for the call of God to me—for my very life.

A DOWNWARD SPIRAL

It seemed that every time I went to a different doctor or specialist in 2001 and 2002, I would receive a new, even more depressing diagnosis. I tried eleven different prescription medications and over sixty-one different supplements (pills, powders, and creams—and these are just the ones I have record of). I went on eight different healthful diets and seventeen grapefruit juice and olive oil gallbladder flushes. I read (and tried to follow the suggestions of) over forty books about different ailments with which I'd been diagnosed. Yet I only seemed to be getting worse.

By the end of the summer of 2003, I had been diagnosed with a multitude of chronic health issues, including:

- laryngopharyngeal reflux disease
- adenomyosis
- Hashimoto's thyroiditis
- low-functioning thyroid
- fibroid tumors
- gallstones
- Epstein-Barr virus
- chronic fatigue syndrome
- chronic bladder infections

- chronic respiratory infections
- depression
- panic attacks

What had started as a slight hoarseness in the back of my throat had blossomed into a full-blown health crisis. Although I was only forty-three years old, my female hormones were at the level of an eighty-year-old woman. I was beyond fatigued twenty-four hours a day. My back and shoulders were racked with pain that never seemed to go away. I battled an almost constant sore throat. I slept for only five fitful hours a night before awakening with my heart pounding and adrenaline coursing through my veins.

During that time, I struggled mightily to handle my normal responsibilities while fighting the never-ending physical symptoms. I described a typical day in my journal entry dated May 2, 2002:

Parents in town. My keyboard player and band director called and quit the worship team. Major stomachache, hoarseness, exhaustion, and insomnia because of stomach pain. Major memory problems. Got lost going to Old Navy then struggled to figure out where I was and what I was doing. Couldn't think straight to give my dad directions to Ray's IGA. When I served dinner, the potatoes and carrots were not done—wish I could blame that on low thyroid! After dinner, my stomach immediately began to hurt.

It still hurt as I was falling asleep and I woke up with it hurting at 3:00 a.m. I got up and ate some millet bread with some almond butter and chamomile tea and took a hot bath. During the hot bath the stomachache went away and I went back to sleep at 5:00 a.m.

Mark did his best to support me during this time. I have a vivid memory of walking through an airport with my husband one day in the middle of 2003. He had arranged to take me away on a trip where I could rest and relax. As we headed toward our gate, I could take only the tiniest of baby steps, inching along through the airport due to pain and fatigue. Meanwhile, Mark carried all the luggage and my purse.

As days of living like this turned into weeks, and weeks of not sleeping turned into months, over the course of three years, I consulted with ten different doctors, searching endlessly for someone who could give me the answers I needed, some sort of hope that I would live a normal life once again. Each time I was given medications that promised to alleviate my symptoms (and that caused different ones), but each time I was told that my conditions were incurable and that I would be forced to battle them for the rest of my life. *How can this be happening to me?* I wondered. I had started an exercise and workout routine a few years earlier, and my weight had never been an issue. I didn't drink, didn't smoke, and I lived a good, moral, healthy life. I was too young to be experiencing these things!

Finally, when one doctor suggested that depression might be part of my problem, I took a questionnaire that showed that, indeed, I was demonstrating symptoms of depression (on top of everything else). I initially thought to myself, *Well, who wouldn't be depressed with a list of ailments like what I am experiencing?*

The doctor suggested that I begin taking an antidepressant to help with my mood. But I couldn't reconcile in my mind how I could possibly be depressed. My rational belief system told me I was living the "good life." I rehearsed the many blessings that I had in my life and I argued with the doctor: "I'm *not* depressed! I have a great life—a husband who loves me, five wonderful children who make good grades and don't get into trouble, and a congregation of people who adore me. What in the world could cause me to be depressed?"

What I didn't know was killing me.

I had no idea at the time, but I was aware only of my superficial reality—the external state of what I could see, feel, hear, taste, and touch. Everything seemed to be well in my external world, except for my physical symptoms, of course. I had achieved what I deemed to be the "perfect life." I was living the American dream—a beautiful family, marriage, home, and career, as well as a personal relationship with a God who loved me and who had died and risen again in order that I might experience this great life. So why was my health in such poor condition? Why was I experiencing so much stress and distress?

What I didn't realize until much later was how subconscious thoughts were affecting my health—that the real world in which I was living was an internal world of fear, hatred, and self-abuse, feelings that had accumulated for years and created patterns of poor emotional management, unhealthy thinking, and negativity. These thoughts were slowly killing me from the inside out.

By the afternoon of August 4, 2003, I had come to the end of my rope. I had been experiencing debilitating panic attacks for over a year. On most occasions, these panic attacks occurred only in front of my husband, but then they began taking place while I was at the church—once during a meeting with some of the worship staff, and then, even more distressing, just before I was to go out on the platform to lead the congregation in praise and worship. I was forced to ask one of my staff members to fill in for me.

Whenever a panic attack came on, I began to cry uncontrollably and irrationally. My breathing increased dramatically until I was hyperventilating, and I literally felt like I was about to die. One day this occurred when my husband and I were dining out in a restaurant, and beyond the distress of the panic attack itself, the humiliation and guilt that I experienced and that I felt I had brought on my husband were almost unbearable. It was a miserable way to live.

For a few months previous to that August, I had been incapacitated with both a bladder infection and a kidney infection. Although I had faithfully been drinking all the good green stuff and eating lots of raw vegetables, I was constantly tired. One doctor ordered an adrenal stress index test, which showed that the level of cortisol and DHEA stress hormones in my body were extremely low. As a result, I had little energy and was on my way to becoming bedridden.

I had always been a very energetic person and a hardworking, homeschooling, worship-leading wife and mother, but I came to the point where I was not able to do even the most basic tasks of a wife and mother—carry a basket of laundry upstairs or stand on my feet to cook a meal. Leading worship became more difficult as well, particularly during those services when Mark decided the worship and praise time should be extended. My husband, who was onstage and singing with me during our worship time, would motion to me to "sing the chorus again"—when all I wanted to do was sit down. I would think to myself, *I can't sing another note; I've got to sit down.* I had always been very expressive and demonstrative while singing and worshiping God, yet now I could barely stand up or raise my hands to God while singing his praise.

HOMEBOUND

My suitcase never did get packed that August day. As I sat in front of it, all the struggles of the past three years came flooding into my mind and I knew I needed help. I could not go on living (or not living) this way.

I cried out to my husband, "I can't do this anymore. I need help. There is something wrong with me. I can't pack this suitcase!"

Helplessly he said, "What do you want me to do?"

Poor guy—I knew there was nothing he could do. He had

already been taking up the slack with the home, kids, and church. The only thing that seemed slightly promising was getting them all out of the house so I could be alone. Was that even a possibility—that Mark and the five kids could go on vacation without me?

But what would people think? That was really my chief concern. What would my parents think? What would our friends whom he was going to visit think? What would the staff of our church think? What would the congregation think? Would they think the pastor and his wife were having marriage problems and taking separate vacations? Would they think I was a weak woman—a hypochondriac with all kinds of imagined illnesses?

Frankly I was so desperately in need of help that I didn't care anymore. *Yes, I have a problem! Yes, I am weak! Yes, I am a failure!* All these thoughts were going through my brain.

Mark and I discussed the situation and decided that the best option under the circumstances would be for him to drive all five children, ages seventeen, fifteen, thirteen, twelve, and five, to South Texas. I don't know how Mark got everyone packed—what seemed overwhelming to me probably wasn't that big of a deal to him—but he eventually got the kids and their suitcases in our car. As my family left on vacation without me, I sat in my bedroom and cried.

At that point I had reached rock bottom, and there was nowhere to go but up. I took the first step toward healing—facing the realization that there was something terribly wrong—something that medications, supplements, and diets couldn't cure. It was something only God could heal, a problem only he could fix.

When my family left, I was completely alone in our house for the first time ever. There were other firsts that week. After two or three days of staying holed up alone, alternating between sleeping and crying, I went to the local video rental store and for the first time picked out videos that *I* liked—as I recall, I picked out five movies based on Jane Austen novels.

That alone was significant. For the last twenty-one years, I had picked out videos that everyone else liked. Now, I could have picked out a video anytime I wanted and told my family, "It's my turn," but that's not the kind of person I was. I found my validation in making everyone else happy, because if I could make them happy, then they would *have* to love me. How could you not love someone who gives up her whole life to do everything for you? (I know—it was sick—but that's where I was living.) Of course, I had *no clue* about this manipulative motivation at the time—no clue.

During that week, I cried several times each day in between trying to sleep and rest. In fact, I cried every day for a whole month after that. Yet I also became determined during that week alone in my house to formulate, with God's guidance, a game plan so that I could position myself for healing. I knew I couldn't *get* healed in that week (if at all), but I knew I had to find a strategy to live the rest of my life. So in addition to sleeping and crying, I consulted with three different doctors that week—still the "same old, same old":

low progesterone, other hormonal imbalances, yeast overgrowth, Epstein-Barr virus.

I cried out to God and said, "Lord, I know there is a way for me to be healed. I know there is!"

I knew and believed all the healing Scriptures in the Bible. I believed that God's will was for me to have an abundant, healthy life. I just didn't know how to get that healing for myself.

"Please, please, Lord," I prayed, "show me the pathway to my healing. I am positive that you know how to heal my body. You made every cell, and you know what has gone wrong and what can heal me. And God, I have to believe that there is someone alive in this world who knows what I need to do to get healed.

"God, I have tried everything I know to do. I have gone to ten different medical doctors and alternative practitioners. I have been on the most popular medications and hormones and supplements, sometimes taking thirty to forty pills a day. I have faithfully been on multiple diets that are supposed to promote healing—the Yeast Diet, the raw foods diet, the Hallelujah Diet, low carb diets, low fat diets. I have done seventeen grapefruit juice and olive oil gallbladder flushes. I have read over forty books to educate myself about causes and cures of all the diagnoses I have received. God, I have been faithfully exercising my body and doing all that I know to do, and yet, Lord, at every doctor's visit, I get a new and more discouraging diagnosis.

"God, I'm asking you to help me. I believe there is

someone out there who knows how my body can be healed, and I'm asking you to somehow bring them across my path. Lord, maybe they live in Asia or Africa, but God, I'm asking you to let me come in contact with them. Lord, maybe they are already dead, but maybe they have written a book that outlines a method of healing. I am asking you to help me get the information I need. I trust you, Lord, and I thank you for your help."

At the end of the week, as my family was returning home, the one thing I knew for sure was that I needed to take a break from my life. Throughout that week alone, I had begun to see the impossibility of continuing or even modifying my current schedule. I needed a new life. I felt like that little hamster in the cage who is running so fast on its wheel but it cannot get off or slow down. My life was so jam-packed that I was beyond managing it or tweaking it. I wanted to scream, "Stop my life; I want to get off!"

AN ANSWER—AND AN UNEXPECTED GIFT

By the time my family came home from vacation, I had made what I considered a radical decision—I was going to take a three-month sabbatical from everything, church duties included, in order to develop a strategy for how I could get my life back on track. At first I was consumed with guilt and fear: *What are people going to think about me? They will realize I'm not perfect!* But I knew that I was too tired to keep up the façade anymore, and I knew that something drastically had to change.

Whereas I had been attending and helping lead five worship experiences per week, now I was going to come to church and sit in the congregation as a regular participant for merely one worship experience per week. I wasn't taking this sabbatical thinking that I could be healed in three months, because I had been told on numerous occasions that I would have to live with these conditions for the rest of my life. I had decided to take a break just to evaluate the condition of my life. I also decided to devote all my energy during these months to trying to discover how either to be healed or to improve the quality of my life while being sick.

Mark made an announcement to the congregation that I was having health challenges and would not be around much for a while. The precious families in our church got together and provided meals for our family every day for three months.

Early on during my sabbatical, as I was in my bathrobe (my new uniform) in the kitchen one morning, my brother Steven called and told me to turn on a local radio station to hear a talk show with a guest whose wife had been healed of illnesses very similar to mine. By the time I hurried to get my boom box, bring it into the kitchen, and tune in to the right frequency, I was able to catch only the last five minutes of the program. Yet I heard enough of the story for a tiny bit of hope to be kindled in me. I went to the website mentioned during the interview and called the organization.

Through my tears, I asked the person on the other end of the phone line, *"Can you help me?"*

He explained that mine was not an easy situation but that he felt there was hope for me to improve.

This organization was not a "Christian" one, per se, although its founder is a Christian and their methods are founded on scriptural principles, but as a counselor from their organization worked with me over the phone each week, I took their methods and combined them with the truths I knew about God.

The Bible tells us: "Do not conform to the pattern of this world, but be transformed by the renewing of your mind" (Romans 12:2, NIV). As I began learning and practicing a type of meditative prayer that enabled me to let go of the lies that had nearly incapacitated me, my life completely changed.

I realize that some Christians are uncomfortable with the idea of meditative prayer, since other belief systems have co-opted the practice of meditation, distancing it from its biblical roots. Yet I quickly discovered that this spiritual discipline is mentioned over and over in Scripture. We're told that Isaac was deep in contemplation the day Rebekah arrived to become his wife: "One evening as he was walking and meditating in the fields, he looked up and saw the camels coming" (Genesis 24:63). When commissioning Joshua to follow Moses as the Israelites' leader, God urged him to obey everything written in the Law. And how could Joshua be certain to do that? God told him to "study this Book of Instruction continually. Meditate on it day and night" (Joshua 1:8).

Furthermore, it's clear that David himself not only meditated but was an enthusiastic advocate of meditative prayer. In Psalm 19:14, he writes, "May the words of my mouth and the meditation of my heart be pleasing to you, O LORD, my rock and my redeemer." In Psalm 145:5, he says, "I will meditate on your majestic, glorious splendor and your wonderful miracles." (See also Psalms 1:2; 27:4; 63:6; 119:23, 27, 48, 52, 117.)

Once I embraced this biblical definition of meditative prayer and began spending time dwelling on the truths of God's love as expressed in Scripture, I experienced peace and a dramatic shift in my emotions almost immediately. After a few weeks, I felt such joy that even though my physical symptoms were unchanged, I would have gladly lived with the symptoms just to know God's love and peace in such a real way.

I didn't fully realize it at the time, but looking back, I see that my mind had been tormented with subconscious lying thought patterns. Meditative prayer began breaking those patterns by enabling me to purposefully reframe situations through the filter of truth, rather than lies. It relieved my mind and body of the stress of the never-ending pounding of negative lying thoughts through the neuropathways of my mind.

During one of our first conversations, my coach took me through what became my first prayer exercise. He told me to find a picture in my mind of someone loving me unconditionally. He said this could be a picture from my past of a time when I had felt completely loved, or it could be an imaginary picture of someone loving me in the way that I wished for.

As the wife of a pastor of a megachurch, I knew there should be plenty of people who loved and cared for me. But sadly I couldn't think of one. I was so deep in depression and despair that despite the fact that I had a beautiful family and a congregation of thousands of people who loved me, all I could feel was that everyone wanted to take, take, take from me. It seemed to me at that time that everyone was constantly demanding something of me—and that I was constantly falling short of their expectations.

With the exception of my deceased grandma and one friend from college whom I hadn't been in contact with for a while, I could not think of one person, including my precious family and many friends, whom I could say I felt truly loved me at that moment.

Then it came to me: there was someone who had always loved me and perhaps loved me still. I closed my eyes and said, softly but without much conviction at first, "Thank you, Lord. Thank you, Lord, for loving me."

Jesus was the only One my troubled mind could know with certainty loved me. But surely he was disappointed in me for my current weakened state, wasn't he? Here I was, in my bathrobe, crying every day, unable to care for my family. Surely God wasn't happy with me, but maybe he did still love me.

My counselor had said to picture someone loving me unconditionally, so I began to let my imagination go to work.

If God really did love me, what would that look like? What kind of picture could I find of God loving me? I decided just to start where I was, on the couch. If I were allowed to use my imagination in this exercise, why couldn't I imagine God with me on the couch? I know that many times in the Bible God was described by the prophets as having arms, hands, feet, and a face.

A picture began to form in my mind: the Father himself was sitting to my right on the couch, right there with me in my bathrobe. While it may seem strange to think of God the Father sitting next to you, picturing him in this way was part of what made the thought so powerful and cut through my "sick" brain. The Bible on many occasions describes God, the creator of the universe, as a father to his children. The prophets even described the bodily features of God, perhaps to help us human beings relate to him.

The idea that God was not just some faraway spirit who loved me from a distance but that he knew me personally and intimately and cared for me was part of what made that love penetrate the neuropathways of my traditional way of viewing God and allowed the power of his love to invade my heart and mind.

Since no one has seen God's face, it wasn't easy picturing him sitting close to me, and yet, if he were truly my father, what would he be doing? I remembered times that my own dad had comforted me as a child. I pictured God, just as my own father, so close to me that his body was touching mine. It felt so good, thinking about him sitting next to me, that

I continued. I imagined his left arm around my shoulder, pulling me close to him.

This thought began to comfort my troubled heart.

Who else loves me? I wondered. The answer came: *Jesus.*

I then began to picture Jesus sitting to my left. He reached out and took my left hand in his, our fingers interlacing like we were intimate friends.

Is there anyone else? Of course—the Holy Spirit. Where would he be? There was an ottoman in front of our sofa—perhaps the Holy Spirit would sit there. Again, picturing the Holy Spirit wasn't easy because . . . he's a spirit! But his personality was so vivid, an old friend who had been with me for a long time and knew me inside and out, encouraging and accepting me.

Then what I saw in my mind's eye completely amazed me. The Holy Spirit, sitting on the ottoman, leaned forward and gently said, *Don't worry, Jennifer. You are going to be fine.* The Father, Son, and Holy Spirit began to comfort me—they assured me they would stay with me forever, right there, with me in my bathrobe, if that was what I needed. They didn't demand that I get up; they didn't demand that I find the faith to get healed. They didn't act impatient, as if they needed to take care of more important or pressing issues—they were simply *there*, resting with me and allowing me the time that I needed in their presence.

If you could have seen me on the couch that day, I would have looked to you as if I were all alone with my hands and fingertips pressed together in front of my lap and my eyes closed as the tears began to flow down my face. But the picture I was seeing was as real to me as the furniture, carpet, and curtains around me. As my body began to respond to the truth that God loved me just the way I was at that moment, that he would never leave me and had never left me, and that he would love me and wait with me for as long as I needed, my body began to respond to these thoughts. I felt relaxed and content. Of course, I did not realize all of this at the time, but this simple outpouring of unconditional love was the catalyst that began to change my life. To this day, whenever I am tempted to feel as if no one loves me, that no one cares, I return to the sofa with the Father, Son, and Holy Spirit, to soak up their love and care for me.

God gave me an unexpected gift during those times of prayer. As much as I love music, I had never written songs before. While being part of a competitive music department in college stretched me in wonderful ways, it also stripped me of some of my self-confidence. By the time I graduated from college, in fact, I was convinced I wasn't really all that talented. I figured I was just second best, perhaps good enough to stand in when necessary. (You can only imagine what kind of stress those negative thoughts caused each week as I prepared to lead worship!)

Now, however, during these prayer times, thoughts in the form of lyrics began to enter my mind as I focused on Scripture and God's truth. I would sit and develop those thoughts for a few minutes, then record them either with a pencil and paper or on my computer. Then later, when I had time, I would take those lyrics, sit at the piano, and hammer out (literally hammer—I hadn't played piano in years!) chords and a melody.

It took me a few months to get the courage to show some of this music to our church's worship staff. Before long, we began teaching some of the songs to the congregation. Then my oldest son, Chris,[1] and other worship team members began writing and sharing their music too. Eventually, we recorded an album called *Unfold*, and we continue to write music today. At the beginning of each chapter, you'll see a few lines from the lyrics that developed as I contemplated God's Word.

After six weeks of this new discipline of meditative prayer, something else amazing happened. At the time, I was still ill, unable to sleep more than five hours each night because I would awaken with heart palpitations. But one evening, I was lying in my bed, about to go to sleep. I had just finished my evening time of meditative prayer when I began to experience a feeling of warmth flowing through my body. It started at the top of my head and streamed down through my neck into my arms and began to flow down through my chest. It felt similar to what I had experienced when I had once taken a very strong prescription muscle relaxer. The last thing I remember thinking was, *Wow, this sure feels good!* Then I must have fallen asleep, because the next thing I knew, I woke up from a restful sleep. When I looked at the clock, I realized that for the first time in months, I had slept for six hours! This may not seem like a big deal to you, but it was huge for me. I woke up feeling wonderful and thought to myself, *I must be getting better!*

I did not mention the warm feeling to my husband but went on with my day. The next two nights I slept seven hours straight. On the third day, I realized that I no longer had any pain in my back and shoulders, nor did I feel fatigued. I told my husband, "I think I have been cured!" And then I told him about the warm feeling that had happened three nights prior. As the day progressed, I became more and more convinced that I was completely free of all symptoms. At church that night, I even got up in front of the church and told them that I had been healed.

That was over seven years ago now, and I am still well. I am not on any prescription medication and take only typical vitamins and supplements. What a contrast to the years when I took thirty to forty pills per day in hopes of alleviating my illnesses and symptoms!

God is so good to me. He loves me and wanted to deliver me from my miserable situation. God loves you so much as well.

My plan is to share what I have learned about the nine Perfect Lies that I believe made me sick. These untruths are some of the most common lies that we humans believe—most every deception that you can think of is a form or derivative of one of these lies. They are "perfect" only in the sense that some of them may seem so real to you that you will want to say, *But Jennifer, that's not a lie—that is true!* I promise you, you can be freed from these self-destructive deceptions by reflecting on the truth. You can find healing for your body, mind, and soul.

Beginning in chapter 4, you will be introduced to each of these nine lies. I will also teach you, step-by-step, how to practice meditative prayer—meditating on the truth, which is the antidote to these lies. I'll also lead you through a specific prayer exercise that can help you combat each of the Perfect Lies. Praying this way will allow you to change and reprogram your thoughts so you are able to live out the truth in your life.

CHAPTER 2

PICTURES ARE POWERFUL!

I was facing death, but now I'm saved.
I can rest again—I'm not afraid.
How kind you are; how good you are;
So merciful, this God of ours.

JENNIFER CROW, "CUP OF SALVATION," 2005

WHEN YOU READ a good novel, what makes it so powerful for you? Is it the way the words fall on the page—the actual ink that is printed on sheets of paper that your eyes happen to scan across? Well, in a way it is. If the words weren't there, you wouldn't be able to understand what was being communicated. But the words *themselves* don't hold the power.

The power to captivate you, to keep you turning to the next page of that book, comes from the pictures the words conjure up in your mind. The more descriptive the words, the more your imagination can take hold and make the story come alive. I believe this is one reason Jesus so often spoke in parables—he knew the word pictures he created would

27

leave more of an impression on people than simply stating the spiritual truths he was trying to convey.

In fact, you probably often think and perceive the world around you as a set of pictures—not just still pictures, but moving pictures. Your brain is designed to take in information constantly through all of your five senses, and as it takes in this data, you translate those details (either consciously or subconsciously) into mental pictures. When you think a thought, you generally are not reading that thought like the words on a page scrolling through the screen of your mind. You are reading that thought by seeing it in pictures in your mind's eye.

Cesare Pavese once said, "We don't remember days; we remember moments"; and that is so true. If you have a disagreement with your boss, you may not remember the exact words that were exchanged, but you will certainly remember the picture of the event created by a combination of the stimuli coming in from your five senses, joined with your emotions and the feelings the words invoked. Or if your husband expresses his love to you by handing you a dozen roses, wrapping his arms around you, and telling you how much you mean to him—which will become a more powerful memory to you: the actual words that he speaks, or the snapshot in your mind of the look on his face, the tone in his voice, and the emotions you felt while he said them?

Throughout your life, you have collected a mental iPhoto file of images and movies that constantly play through your brain whether you want them to or not—many times seemingly uncontrolled by you. Sometimes they come inadvertently or subconsciously when you least expect them. They are so subconscious that most times you are not even *aware* of them! The brain has a tendency to group like things together to draw conclusions. That's why these pictures can be triggered by a smell or other stimuli. Most often, though, they are triggered when you experience a similar emotion.

Thoughts and emotions, then, are the foundation of the Perfect Lies. That's why, as I introduce each lie in the upcoming chapters, I'll begin by listing some of the thoughts and feelings that often go along with that lie.

Keep in mind that there are six basic human emotions. All other emotions are variables of these:

- anger
- disgust
- fear
- happiness
- sadness
- surprise

God gave us these emotions to help us navigate our environment. In that respect, they are similar to our five physical senses; in fact, I like to think of them as our six emotional senses. Just as our physical senses of sight, smell, taste, touch, and hearing help us interpret our environment, so emotions help us respond quickly and appropriately to our environment.

For example, if you hear a bloodcurdling scream in the next room, your body—in a split second without conscious thought—feels both fear and surprise. Those emotional responses jolt your nervous system into action and get your adrenaline pumping, which sends blood to your large muscles so you can immediately spring into action. The emotion you feel is neither positive nor negative; it is a signal to help you navigate your environment.

God didn't fashion our bodies to constantly live at a heightened state of alert, however, which is why emotions are generally temporary or fleeting. You may feel a strong burst of emotion at one point, but then several minutes or hours later, you no longer feel that emotion. Of course, there are exceptions, as when a loved one passes away or when you're in the first stages of falling in love.

People get into trouble when they either suppress their emotions or when their emotions, which are intended to be temporary, smolder for too long. Emotions need to be able to come and go to give our bodies rest from the physical responses of emotions. When you live by a Perfect Lie, however, unhealthy emotions—along with inaccurate thoughts—may persist.

THE MAKING OF A STRONGHOLD

Perhaps like me, you remember getting in trouble as a child. I remember stealing Christmas decorations out of a neighbor's garage, lying to my teacher, and keeping a bracelet I found on the playground. My parents punished me for a few of these offenses, but whether I was caught or not, I responded to such situations by concluding that I was a bad little girl. While still a child, this had become a well-worn thought pattern. Even when someone incorrectly accused me of doing something wrong, the neuropathway was quick to grab that thought and add it to the "You are a bad girl" file. Before I knew it, a huge component of my thinking was slanted toward the lie "You are bad."

In her book *Who Switched Off My Brain?*, Dr. Caroline Leaf takes an entire chapter to describe the anatomy of a thought and another chapter to describe the growth of a thought. She explains that each thought in our brain is made up of a treelike nerve cell with multiple branches called dendrites, over which impulses travel. The more branches there are on a "tree," the more prolific and accessible the thought will be. A thought can be true or false, but every time we dwell on it, that thought develops and more branches are added. A thought that is frequently and familiarly accessed can become a hugely complex tangle of neuron cells and dendrite branches that literally becomes rooted in a person's psyche.[2]

THE WHOLE TRUTH AND NOTHING BUT . . .

Our complex thought processes sometimes make it difficult for us to put our trust in God's promises. In Jeremiah 29:11-13, for instance, the Lord expresses how he feels about you (and about me) personally:

I know what I'm doing. I have it all planned out—
plans to take care of you, not abandon you, plans
to give you the future you hope for. When you call
on me, when you come and pray to me, I'll listen.
When you come looking for me, you'll find me. Yes,
when you get serious about finding me and want it
more than anything else, I'll make sure you won't be
disappointed. (THE MESSAGE)

This Scripture is one of many that clarify the truth of God's great love for us. Some people have been raised to believe that God is a big, bad ogre up in the sky who is ready to whack them over the head with a baseball bat every time he catches them doing something wrong. One of the goals of this book is to correct that false assumption about God and to help you see the truth of his nature. God has great things planned for us, and he wants us to pursue those plans with our entire being—to search for him and the future he's planned for us!

Jesus himself spent his whole life explaining and showing by example what God is like and how he thinks and feels about us, his children. Now, I've known since I was young that the Bible says that all of us have fallen short and missed the mark but that, as followers of Christ, we have been forgiven and our sins cast away as far as the east is from the west. I have even taught others this truth; still, even as an adult I couldn't shake the overpowering subconscious thought pattern: *You are bad.*

The problem was that even though I had received and acknowledged God's forgiveness, which began to create a new thought pattern in my brain, this "tree" was just a seedling and was dwarfed by the one that told me I wasn't good enough.

Though he wasn't aware of the science behind it, when the apostle Paul refers to "strongholds" in 2 Corinthians 10:4, I believe he is referring to a scientific truth: these nerve cells can form the basis of our strongholds. He wrote:

> The weapons we fight with are not the weapons of the world. On the contrary, they have divine power to demolish strongholds. We demolish arguments and every pretension that sets itself up against the knowledge of God, and we take captive every thought to make it obedient to Christ. (2 Corinthians 10:4-5, NIV)

Notice that Paul uses the words *strongholds*, *arguments*, and *pretension* as synonyms for false or lying thoughts.

Every thought can grow and develop as more data is added to the thought. Let's take the thought, *I am a bad girl and I deserve to be rejected*, and look at its growth in the life of a forty-year-old woman. As a little girl, when she first had that thought, there was a picture in her mind associated with it. The image might have been of a time she disobeyed or disappointed her parents by crying or throwing a tantrum. Perhaps she was not only punished for it but was also given the silent treatment.

This thought of her unworthiness began as a tiny neuron with very few branches. But as she grew and entered adulthood, she found herself in countless situations where a teacher, a friend, or a family member was unhappy with her and withdrew from her. Even if she had done nothing to cause the conflict, her brain might automatically have attributed the situation to her belief that *I am a bad girl and I deserve to be rejected*. Each time that happened, another branch was added and additional pictures collected to build upon that thought or belief.

Finally that thought had become a huge tree in her mind, and she added branches to it whenever an experience reinforced it. She probably could not tell you how this thought started or the initial picture associated with it. All she knows is that her thoughts seem to run toward this conclusion whenever she experiences conflict.

SEEING THE FOREST AMONG THE TREES

Think of the number of images that are stored in your mind from your childhood. You have around 100 trillion of these "trees" in your brain, and each one is capable of growing up to seventy thousand branches. Many of those images were filtered through your perception as a toddler, a preschooler, an elementary-aged child, an adolescent, or a teenager. How an event played out from your perspective as a child might be completely different from the way you would see it if the same events took place today, now that you are an adult. Yet you continue to process similar situations through the perspective of a child because that is when those "branches" formed.

In truth, many of these images, which your brain considers factual, are really distortions of the truth—framings of your reality and how you perceived it at one moment in time. Let's say you are forty-five years old but you still play over and over mental pictures of your father verbally abusing you, either in your subconscious or even your conscious mind. Perhaps the picture is accompanied by his taunt *You're stupid* or *You'll never amount to anything*. Perhaps these internal pictures have affected your self-image all your life because you believed them.

You were only a child at the time when your dad berated you—of course you would have had a tendency to believe what an adult, an authority figure, told you. But your father was only twenty-two years old when these events happened. If a twenty-two-year-old were verbally abusing you today, what would you do or think? You would probably think something like, *Get out of my face* (in the nicest possible way). *You don't know what you're talking about—forget you!*

And yet today, your brain neuropathways have been structured around images that are not accurate representations of your current reality. If it feels as if you have been programmed to think a certain way, the truth is, you have! You have some faulty programming in your brain caused by these destructive lies, which are stored in the form of distorted pictures. Perhaps your behavior is still being controlled thirty years later by a twenty-two-year-old kid who may have been doing the best he could but probably didn't know how to speak the truth.

The point is that many of the thought pictures currently stored in your brain and heart are based on lies—lies that can make you sick, depressed, and crippled in your ability to live freely as God designed you to live.

In this book, I identify nine common lies that are recognized as destructive by mental health professionals and the Bible—lies that virtually every human being in the world is tempted to believe. You might read these lies and say, *But those aren't lies. They are true about me.* That is the very nature of a lie. It is a thought so deceitful and credible that you accept it as truth.

I found myself in the same situation. The lies I believed were so ingrained into my very being that I accepted them as a part of me. I thought they were a part of my DNA, my very humanity. They were like a symbiotic parasite that actually seemed to become a part of the host. I could not separate my lying thoughts from the truth, and I didn't realize that I had internalized them from a young age. My lying thoughts (which I accepted as truth) *were* me. If this sounds like something from a crazy sci-fi movie, get ready, because sometimes truth is stranger than fiction.

Before scientists ever knew about brain neuropathways or psychology, the apostle Paul wrote:

Do not conform to the pattern of this world, but be transformed by the renewing of your mind.

Then you will be able to test and approve what
God's will is—his good, pleasing and perfect will.
(Romans 12:2, NIV)

My version of Romans 12:2 could be worded as follows:

Do not be controlled anymore by the pictures in
your mind from your past experiences, which create
neuropathways in your brain based on lies, but
instead, have your mind reprogrammed by changing
the pictures of your heart and mind to reflect the
truth—God's truth about you. Then you will be able
to recognize a lie when you see it, and you will be
able to know the difference between lies and truth
and be able to discern God's good, pleasing, and
perfect will for you.

The wrong patterns of your thoughts (your brain's neuropathways), which have been based on the perceived images
of your past, must be reprogrammed or transformed by the
renewing of your mind.

I have learned a concrete way to renew my mind. It
is simple to do, easy to understand, and very effective. It
requires some time, effort, and discipline, but it takes only
a few minutes each day. It works so well that after imple-
menting this system for six weeks, my mind was no longer jumping immediately to faulty pictures and the lies that
accompanied them. At last I found relief from the constant

stress my body had been under so that my body was able to function as God intended, which was to fight disease and infection through my immune system. My body began to get rid of impurities and to be nourished effectively through my digestive system and other bodily systems. My body began to work properly and I began to be healed.

As I have said before, I am now in great health and not on any prescription medication. But more than that, I am happy and I am whole. I love myself. I accept myself just the way I am, even with all of my faults and failures. I enjoy every day. I have compassion for others instead of antagonism. I do not mean to say that I never battle these same lies, because I have found those thoughts can easily begin to grow again. But now I have effective tools and a strategy for the fight. My life has been completely transformed by the process of learning how to renew my mind.

CHAPTER 3

WHAT IS THE TRUTH?

I am yours. I've always been.
From the moment you first knew me 'til the end.
'Til the end of time I'll always be
The one you love. You gave your life for me.

JENNIFER CROW, "IT'S OKAY," 2005

WHEN I WAS FIRST ILL, I would walk by piles of dirty laundry or a messy room and tell myself, *You are a bad housekeeper.* Virtually every time my children fought or talked back to me or their father, another subconscious thought would scold me: *If you were a good mother, your children would be better behaved.* When church staff or worship team members had a dispute, this critical thought would form in my mind: *If you were more spiritually mature, your staff wouldn't be having these problems.*

I was drowning in hidden allegations from Satan that it was my responsibility to save, organize, and fix the world—especially for my loved ones. Because I wasn't doing that, I was bad, not good enough. For a time, I took these negative

39

internal critiques as beatings that made me work harder, try harder! But no matter how hard I tried, my efforts to make my world perfect always seemed to come up short.

The constant stream of negative messages did nothing but pull me down and eventually took a toll on my health and relationships. It was like beating a dead horse: no matter how hard you beat the horse, it is *not* going to get up. Sadly, I was unaware that I was controlled by Perfect Lies.

Not only that, but I operated from a prideful knowledge that often set me up as the judge and jury. Who needed God when they had me to tell them what was right and wrong? I was so quick to say, "That's right. That's wrong. He should do that. She shouldn't do this." Sometimes I thought I was so smart that I didn't need God's help, and I tried to push through life in my own power using my own "brilliant" ideas. I began to play God, thinking I must legislate what each person in my world was doing.

This type of thinking was a recipe for stress and burnout, since I began to feel that the weight of the world was on my shoulders instead of on God's, where it belongs. God gave people a free will to choose. I needed to recognize that I could give people that free will to interact as they chose. I was only responsible for what *I* chose.

THE FATHER OF LIES

Let's go back to the beginning to see where these lies originated. For you see, humanity has not always been plagued and tempted by the lies of the devil. Yes, you have heard of him—the devil, the guy in the red suit with horns and a pitchfork. Well, the horns and pitchfork probably originated from Saturday morning children's cartoons or some medieval artist's imagination. But the actual devil is real, not imaginary. Jesus mentioned the devil and the place prepared for him, hell, many times.

One of the clearest passages is when Jesus described him as a liar and the father of lies: "He [the devil] was a murderer from the beginning. He has always hated the truth, because there is no truth in him. When he lies, it is consistent with his character; for he is a liar and the father of lies" (John 8:44).

Many people have difficulty believing that there is an actual devil loose in the universe, wreaking havoc in the lives of both nonbelievers and believers alike. But the Bible says that it is true. Lucifer himself, one of God's most magnificent angelic creatures, had been in charge of worship of the Most High God. At some point, however, he became filled with pride and desired to take the place of God on the throne (see Isaiah 14:12-14)—that is why Lucifer was cast out of heaven. Destined for eternal torment, Satan would like nothing more than to destroy us, too. And he would like to demolish all of the wonderful plans God has for us, just as he tried to do in my own life. We are in a battle, and our greatest weapon against the enemy is the truth of God's Word.

In John 10:10, Jesus contrasted God's original plan for humanity with the devil's schemes: "The thief's purpose is to steal and kill and destroy. My purpose is to give them a rich and satisfying life."

God's original plans to give us abundant lives are evident in the opening chapters of Genesis, which tell of the creation of the world and the lives of Adam and Eve in the Garden of Eden. Before Satan entered the picture, life was literally "heaven on earth."

If Adam and Eve became hungry, they could just go to the nearest bush and grab some berries. They had all the fresh water they needed right there as well. In fact, the book of Genesis says that four rivers flowed through the Garden, providing fresh, clean, drinkable water.

Everything was easy for Adam and Eve—they didn't have to exert a lot of blood, sweat, and tears to get their food and shelter like we do. They had fulfilling work, which was challenging, interesting, and mentally stimulating. I can imagine Eve saying to Adam each day, "Time to wake up, sweetie. Let's eat our breakfast. Here's your papaya. Now let's go out and see what new animals we can find today." Their entire job in life was discovering God's magnificent creation and learning what new things God had made for them in their world. It was fulfilling and creative work . . . and it was fantastic.

Besides having a great physical environment, Adam and Eve had total, unmasked intimacy with their Creator. Every single day, the Bible says, they walked and talked with God in the cool of the day. Every day. In the flesh. Instant access. God was not hidden from them. They were there together, every day of their lives.

They had a fulfilling marital relationship. Adam had a wife who totally understood him because she was from his own body. Eve knew what Adam wanted and what he liked, and vice versa, because they were one flesh. They were totally compatible in every way.

Try to imagine it if you can: no sickness, no disease, no fear, no anger—not even the concept of any of these things. Best of all, there was no idea of death, of separation or brokenness of any kind, because these things were not in God's original plan for mankind.

They could have lived that way forever. But something happened.

God gave Adam and Eve the world to rule over, and he gave them a free will to choose what they wanted. He gave them every tree in the Garden to eat from, with only one restriction. He told them there was *one tree* in the Garden from which they must not eat. They had the whole world, except for that *one little tree*. Why does the grass always seem greener on the other side, and why do we have a tendency to focus on that one thing that we can't have?

Unfortunately, God's good plans were twisted the moment sin entered the world. Let's take a look and see how it happened.

The serpent was the shrewdest of all the wild animals the LORD God had made. One day he asked the woman, "Did God really say you must not eat the fruit from any of the trees in the garden?"

"Of course we may eat fruit from the trees in the garden," the woman replied. "It's only the fruit from the tree in the middle of the garden that we are not allowed to eat. God said, 'You must not eat it or even touch it; if you do, you will die.'"

"You won't die!" the serpent replied to the woman. "God knows that your eyes will be opened as soon as you eat it, and you will be like God, knowing both good and evil."

The woman was convinced. She saw that the tree was beautiful and its fruit looked delicious, and she wanted the wisdom it would give her. So she took some of the fruit and ate it. Then she gave some to her husband, who was with her, and he ate it, too. At that moment their eyes were opened, and they suddenly felt shame. (Genesis 3:1-7)

We soon learn that the snake was actually Satan, or Lucifer, in disguise. The evil one was determined to deceive the creatures God had made in his own image. But why did Eve so easily succumb to temptation? Why did she allow Satan even the smallest foothold into the Paradise in which she and her husband were living? It's the same reason you and I have trouble realizing our own "heaven on earth," the blessings God wants us to experience right now: we believe the devil's lies. We believe them because they *sound so true, so reasonable*. Perhaps the devil has even tempted you as he tempted Eve with statements like the following:

- Did God really say . . . ? (God is holding something out on you. You're missing out!)

- You won't really die if you eat this piece of fruit. (God is not trustworthy; when he says something, it may or may not take place.)

- Your eyes will be opened; you will experience great pleasure when you eat this. (Doing things God's way will not bring you the results you want out of life.)

- You will become just like God—knowing the difference between good and evil. (You don't really need God; you can do everything on your own without his help.)

The lies Satan told Eve are the same lies he told me, and very likely, the same lies he is trying to convince you to believe right now.

Because Adam and Eve believed Satan's lies, the entire universe is under a curse and under the temporary rule of Satan until Christ returns to defeat him once and for all. Humanity is still vulnerable to the power of Satan's lies, and sin is inevitable when we believe the lies of the devil rather than the promises of the good God who created us.

I accepted Christ when I was young and began to understand his love for me. I really wanted to please God and obey him, so I never smoked a cigarette, got drunk, or took drugs. Satan was going to have a hard time tempting me to steal, cheat, or murder either. But I completely bought into some of Satan's other lies!

Fortunately, God did not leave you or me alone to be tortured by these lies; he sent his own Son to earth to give us a way of escape from the power of the Perfect Lies and the sin that they bring. Jesus, God's Son, revealed the truth to us. The truth is that God loves us still, even though we are so weak with temptation that we have given the devil power in our lives.

When Jesus came to earth, he also was tempted by Satan to believe lies. Because he refused, Jesus was like a second Adam—he came to give us a new start. He was worthy and able to take the punishment we deserve, so that when Jesus was put to death on the cross, the penalty for our sin was paid in full. He also broke the power of death so that all people who accept this gift and repent of believing the lies and acting on them will actually never die. Yes, their bodies will die, but their souls and spirits will go to heaven. Just as Jesus' body was raised on the third day after his death, so our bodies will be resurrected to live with Jesus and God forever on the new earth. Creation will be back to the way God designed it: men and women walking and talking together with their God on the new earth, ruling and reigning for all of time.

I stand as a walking, talking miracle of what God can do when a person dares to persevere and realizes, *There must be more to life than this!* As I began to recognize the lies Satan was using to hoodwink me and hijack God's plans for my life, I began to combat them with the truth of God's Word. (Like Jesus, in other words, I learned to fight the temptation of accepting lies by immersing myself in the truth found in God's Word.) And I employed the process of visual imagery in meditative prayer—drawing on pictures in my mind and my imagination to help sink the vital, healing truths of Scripture deep into my heart, where true faith could be birthed.

That doesn't mean that I am perfect or that I don't still struggle on a daily basis. However, I understand God's love for me in a deeper, more personal way. I am better able to take him at his Word and to say, "No more!" to the deceptions of the enemy.

DEFEATING PERFECT LIES

When we believe one of the devil's lies, it infiltrates our entire lives—every cell of our being, spirit, soul, and body—and it can make us sick in every way, physically, emotionally, mentally, and spiritually.

When we accept Satan's lies, we actually believe a certain picture about ourselves—a mental image that has been "programmed" into our thoughts. We believe in and imagine as true a picture of ourselves, or our marriage, or our health that is contradictory to God's Word. I've identified nine of these Perfect Lies, which we will examine more closely throughout this book. As we examine these tools of the enemy, it will be important for you to learn to renew your mind (following 2 Corinthians 5:17 and Romans 12:1-2), allowing your confession of the truths of Scripture to penetrate not just your thoughts, in word form, but also to transform your heart, through the pictures and images the Holy Spirit reveals to you.

I'm excited to begin this journey with you! Let's get started!

CHAPTER 4

PERFECT LIE NUMBER ONE: I AM UNLOVABLE

I MUST MEET THE STANDARDS OTHERS HAVE SET FOR ME
BECAUSE OTHERWISE I WILL BE UNLOVABLE.

There is no hurt so deep you cannot feel.
There is no heart so cold you cannot heal the pain.
Your blood flows down, revives my soul.
I am drowning in this love that makes me whole.

CHRIS CROW AND JENNIFER CROW, "REDEEMED," 2007

THE DAY HAD finally arrived—my fourth birthday! My mom had invited all of my neighbor friends and her friends' children to a birthday party. In spite of my parents' limited financial resources, she had put her heart and soul into making this day special. She made adorable hand-crafted decorations and bought me a new dress, covered by a crisp white pinafore.

My grandmother had driven from Houston to Silsbee, Texas, the night before so she'd have time to create a round cake featuring a make-believe carousel. Animal-shaped cookies danced around the edges, and they were attached by colorful ribbons to the carousel's center candy pole. She even decorated a beautiful design on the cake using tiny silver candy balls, which I was sure were made of real silver, but you could eat them!

Although my mom had her hands full with my little brother, who had just turned two, she used her natural organizational abilities to plan everything to the nth degree. She set up the table and games outside under our carport, since our tiny two-bedroom house wasn't big enough for all those children and moms. There was so much excitement in the air, I could hardly stand it!

Finally the guests arrived, carrying colorful packages with bright ribbons and bows. Right about then, things started going downhill. My mom asked everyone to sit down and pointed me to the head of the table. I protested that I wanted to sit by my friends. She wouldn't hear of it, and I started to cry. Then Mom started serving everyone else pieces of that delicious-looking cake and told me I'd be the last one served because I was the hostess and needed to serve my guests first. I started wailing. The same thing happened when the punch was served. My mother, struggling to maintain control, tried to explain to me the rules of proper party decorum.

When it was time to play games, I wanted to go first because, after all, it was my party! Mom insisted that I go last and told me she couldn't believe how rudely I was acting.

I remember thinking, *What kind of party is this where the birthday girl is treated worse than everyone else?*

Finally the moment I had been waiting for all day came: it was time to open the presents! My excitement turned to ecstasy as each gift I opened seemed so much better than the last one. Just as I finished opening the last one, my mother began whisking them away to be hidden until the guests left. That was the *last straw*! I wanted my toys and I wanted them *now*!

My mother was extremely angry. My behavior had put a damper on the entire party. I just couldn't seem to control myself. Every time my mother reprimanded me for my bad behavior, I heard her and I wanted to please her, but I thought, *It's just not fair!*

In fact, my behavior and her response became my predominant memory of the party. I couldn't remember any of the wonderful details of that day without feeling guilt and shame. Every time I thought of it, I felt sick to my stomach. For days, weeks, months—and even years, it seemed—when we would reminisce about the party, my mom would say, "Do you remember how terrible you acted?" In my mind, that translated to *Because of the way you misbehaved, you are unlovable and now everybody knows it.*

Of course, the scenario I've described seems fairly benign; it certainly wasn't very earth shattering. There was nothing atypical or abnormal about the situation. My mother was doing what she thought was right—trying to teach me to be a polite and respectful young lady who could handle herself well in social situations. She was not trying to convince me that I was unlovable. In fact, she has demonstrated her great love for me many times since then. For my part, I was acting exactly as you might expect a four-year-old with no clue about birthday party etiquette to act. Yet I fell victim to a lie that has plagued the entire human race: I am unlovable.

My attempts to please at any cost were a reflection of a very basic desire—one I share with you and every other person. I longed to be fully loved and accepted. This quest for acceptance begins at birth and ideally is filled by our parents. The truth, however, is that not one of us was born into a perfect family—no matter how much we may wish we had been. First, every child is imperfect and struggles with selfish notions from birth; second, all mothers and fathers are imperfect human beings, with hurts and hang-ups of their own that prevent them from loving their children exactly the way they should.

Kathy found that out after beginning a parenting class at her church. She explained to her six-year-old daughter, Kayla, that she was taking a course to help her be a better mommy. The following Sunday, Kayla became upset and had a tantrum because she was not getting her way. Both parents tried to calm her, but with tears streaming down her face, Kayla announced to her mother, "You told me you were taking a course to make you a better mommy. Well, it's not working!"

No matter how wonderful your mom and dad were,

chances are there were times when they snapped at you in anger or punished you unfairly or simply weren't there for you when you needed their love and attention.

Or maybe you came from an abusive home, one in which your parents harmed you because of their own rage or sexual addictions. Perhaps your parents didn't hurt you physically but spoke painful words that have echoed in your spirit for years. Your dad or mom may have had to work long hours in order to keep the family afloat, so they just weren't able to give you the time you needed. Divorce and abuse, anger and unforgiveness, harsh words and broken promises are the reality for many children. Maybe that is what took place in the home in which you grew up.

Whatever the case, because we all are the children of imperfect parents, we have grown up with some feelings of hurt or the painful absence of love when we needed it. And our enemy, the devil, loves to take these feelings and pervert them into his first lie:

I must meet the standards others have set for me because otherwise I will be unlovable.

Have you ever had this thought or feeling? Probably not in so many words. But does it ever seem that no matter what you do, it is never enough to satisfy those around you? Do you feel as if you have to perform in order to gain the approval of other people—that you must do everything perfectly to maintain the love of your family and friends?

Lies closely related to this could be *I am insignificant* or *I am flawed* or *What I think or feel has no value*.

If you believe this lie, you may have a recorded message in your mind that is always accusing you through questions and statements like these:

> *Can't you do anything right?*
> *What is wrong with you?*
> *You are a failure!*
> *How can you think or feel that way?*

Perhaps these thoughts echo what your parents, teachers, or others have said to you in the past. If you were ever chastised with the words, "How many times do I have to tell you . . . ?" you may be a prime candidate for believing the lie that you are unlovable unless your actions meet the approval of others. And chances are, you are experiencing feelings of guilt, insignificance, and even resentment and unforgiveness toward those who have hurt you.

This lie is so insidious that it's possible to start believing it even before you are old enough to speak. I recall one of the first times I believed this lie. Even though I was deathly afraid of the water, my parents decided to sign me up for swimming lessons. They encouraged me, bribed me, shamed me, and tried everything else they could think of to help their little daughter overcome her fear of drowning. This situation proved to be a terrible quandary for me, though, because my greatest fear—above all others—was the fear of not being loved.

I desperately sought my parents' approval, and the fear of losing their love drove my most basic instincts, thoughts, attitudes, and actions. Because of that, I was in a bit of a pickle; I had to decide which was greater—my fear of the water or my fear of disappointing others. I don't remember much about my swimming teacher, Mrs. Deer, except that she was a kind, warm body to hug, even in her wet bathing suit. I agonized about pleasing her, too, and one day finally blurted out to my mother, "Mama, will Mrs. Deer still love me even if I never put my face under the water?"

My poor mother was at her wit's end, and even though she herself did not believe in the power of prayer, she decided to try it as a last resort. "Jennifer," she said, "would you like for us to pray that God would help you not be afraid of the water?" I was open to anything at that point and agreed—and we said a little prayer for courage so I could overcome this fear.

The next day of swimming lessons came around, as I knew it would (I had been dreading it, as always), but I knew what I had to do. I told Mrs. Deer that this was the day I would put my face under the water because Mama had prayed that I'd be able to. She held me at the surface of the water, and I took a huge breath, as if my very life depended on it. Then I plunged my head into the cold, impenetrable darkness of the water while other children splashed happily around me. My face was wet for one split second before I emerged, sputtering but triumphant! I had done it! I felt like a mighty princess who had just conquered the fiercest dragon—even though my mother told me later I'd barely let my nose break the surface of the water and my hair hadn't even gotten wet. That didn't matter, however—it was a huge victory for me, and the first of many experiences in my life when I had to battle, and overcome, the lies of the enemy.

Looking back on this situation from the perspective of a rational adult, it is difficult to understand what the big deal was. Mrs. Deer was certainly not concerned or probably even thinking about whether she loved me. She was teaching a class, doing a job. And so what if Mrs. Deer *didn't* love me? What do I care? I don't recall ever seeing Mrs. Deer again once those lessons were over. Why would I put that much emotional energy into silly worry about what a virtual stranger thought?

My point is this—in my little four-year-old brain, I believed a lie: I am unlovable if I don't _____ (put my head under the water, make good grades, act right, etc.). You can fill in the blank for your own life! When the lie that you are lovable only if you meet the expectations of others goes unchecked, it becomes a stronghold in your mind that is difficult to break because you will gather so much "evidence" to sustain this lie.

Emotions associated with this lie

- *feelings of insignificance*
- *resentment*
- *unforgiveness*

LIE DETECTOR TEST

Ask yourself the following questions to determine if you have believed the first Perfect Lie: *I must meet the standards others have set for me because otherwise I will be unlovable.*

- How did your parents treat you when you did something wrong as a child? Was your mistake easily forgiven and forgotten, or held over your head?
- Do you ever feel as if you need to perform in order to gain the love and approval of those around you? the love and approval of God?
- What kinds of things do you say to yourself when you make a mistake or fail at a task? Are you affirmative or disapproving with yourself?

So many people walk around today wearing masks—especially in the church. They are afraid to show their true selves—to admit that they are not perfect, that they have sinned, both in the past and in the present. You may be thinking to yourself, *Yep, Jennifer, that's me. I am unlovable.* Let me clarify something. You may have made serious mistakes and messed up, but that does not mean you are not lovable!

As a young youth pastor's wife, I struggled to maintain the illusion that I was a spiritual leader. I didn't feel spiritual, and I certainly didn't feel that I measured up to the dynamic women in ministry who were on staff at the large megachurch where my husband was employed. They seemed so perfect and full of faith, never seeming to make any mistakes. I was fearful to let anyone know of my internal daily struggles with raising my children, being a young wife, arguing with my husband, and not reading my Bible because I had been up nursing the baby all night. Since I didn't have the courage to share my struggles, I began to feel alienated and ashamed. Finally all of this built up to the point that I couldn't take it anymore.

One Sunday, I was sitting in the second row in church, and as I heard the pastor preaching, I began to feel so desperate to get help that I decided to throw off the façade and "come clean." My heart was beating fast and my palms were sweating, but I was so miserable, I didn't care what anyone thought. I, the megachurch youth pastor's wife, got up out of my seat in front of five thousand people and responded to the altar call for prayer. Well, you might not think that was a big deal, but the call for prayer was for people who battled demon possession! All the older ladies on staff quickly came to my rescue and surrounded me and prayed for me. I'm not sure what they really thought, but they seemed to support the demon-possessed youth pastor's wife's prayer request for deliverance! No, I obviously was not demon possessed, but I use this example to show you that sometimes in our minds, we live behind a false wall of shame created from the lie *I am unlovable*. By the way, my experience that morning was a defining moment in my life. I summoned up the nerve to fight my fear of not measuring up and risked others' disapproval by asking for help. Doing so has given me courage to publicly and privately acknowledge my imperfections in spite of apprehension many times since then.

God never meant for us to live in hiding and in shame—that is one reason Jesus attacked hypocritical people so vigorously. Jesus placed *love*—for God, for others, and for oneself—before anything else. The lie that we are lovable only if we meet others' expectations is a distortion of the truth, with just enough veracity thrown in to make it seem believable. After all, God has not done away with standards for right living. At the same time, he reminds us, "The LORD is like a father to his children, tender and compassionate to those who fear him. For he knows how weak we are; he remembers we are only dust" (Psalm 103:13-14). He provides his power to help us live the way he planned from the beginning. That doesn't change when we fail. Because of his sacrificial work on the cross, we can experience grace and love that "covers a multitude of sins" (1 Peter 4:8).

ANTIDOTE TO THE FIRST PERFECT LIE

When my brother and I were growing up in the '70s, we watched *Batman* on TV after school (when I was supposed to be practicing piano!). Batman frequently got himself into one mess after another while trying to fight the evil villains. Quite often, one of the villains would play a magic trick on him, making him eat a food or injecting a poison that would either incapacitate Batman or make him act completely crazy and unlike himself. Just before he plunged to his death, walked into a trap, or killed one of the good guys, his trusty sidekick, Robin, would get him the antidote that had to be quickly created with a certain herb from a certain obscure plant. Or even better, Batman and Robin would take the Universal Drug Antidote Pill that would protect them from being vulnerable to the evils of the Joker, Two-Face, and Poison Ivy!

That was obviously just a cheesy TV show, but the truth in real life is this: for every Perfect Lie that has been ingrained into the fabric of who we are, there is an antidote, solution, or truth that counters that lie. These antidotes are not a closely guarded secret, nor did I make them up. All of them are found in the Bible.

One of the key components to my healing and the renewing of my mind and thoughts has been meditative prayer. Although you can focus on many things during your time with the Lord, some of which I will outline in later chapters, focusing and meditating on a specific Scripture verse is foundational.

You may be thinking, *Well, I already know the Bible. Is this book just going to give me Scripture verses for every lie?*

Reading a few verses isn't enough. I knew the Bible very well by the time I became so ill. For heaven's sake, I was a leader in our church! I proclaimed truth through word and song, but for some reason I was bound by numerous wrong thoughts that had become strongholds in my life. I am not just going to give you the antidote, but I am going to teach you and show you how to apply it.

Let's say you have a minor disagreement with one of your siblings or a close friend. When that person gets short with you, you flare up in anger and say something mean spirited. Once you have calmed down and are going about your day, you feel condemned and guilty about your behavior. You think of how frustrated you were when you lashed out. You don't feel good, and you can't help but conclude that your sister, brother, or friend doesn't love you. You know you were wrong to be so rude.

Now of course you need to apologize to the person you have wronged. But how do you get over that feeling of being unworthy of love? Because if you don't get over that, you will go through the whole day, the whole next day, and the whole *next* day feeling condemned and unlovable. You may know that, with time, you will gradually forget how bad you feel right then and might even start feeling a little bit better. But as soon as you speak rashly again, all that guilt, rejection, and shame will come back. That poison is still in your system if you have internalized this lie.

How do you get rid of the self-condemnation? Here's what I have found: if I counter that lie with the truth of God's Word and meditate on the passage until I begin to believe it, then the very fabric of my brain and thought system will begin to change. For me, meditative prayer means focusing and praying on a truthful picture from Scripture and doing so in short but frequent spurts throughout the day.

So let's find the antidote to the first lie: *I must meet the standards others have set for me because otherwise I will be unlovable.*

We don't have to go far to find an antidote to this lie. Let's consider John 3:16, perhaps the best-known Scripture verse in the entire Bible, and possibly one of the least appreciated.

> God loved the world so much that he gave his one and only Son, so that everyone who believes in him will not perish but have eternal life. God sent his Son into the world not to judge the world, but to save the world through him. (John 3:16-17)

Many people stop reading after these two verses, but the next verse also contains an important truth:

> There is no judgment against anyone who believes in him. (John 3:18)

When you read that Scripture, what comes to mind? Read it again—out loud—and think about what you are seeing in your mind's eye as you read it. Renewing your mind requires more than mentally assenting to a truth. Reprogramming the neuropathways in your brain requires forging new paths and thought processes. This can be done through the use of thought pictures. Yet not just any picture will do.

To illustrate, let me tell you the picture that John 3:16 conjured up in my mind when I first heard it as a child in Sunday school. Perhaps we were singing the song "He's Got the Whole World in His Hands" that day, but for some reason when I thought of the words, "God loved the world so much that he gave . . . ," I saw a large green-and-blue world floating in black outer space with the stars of the galaxy twinkling around it. In my mind, I also saw giant hands wrapped around it.

Though this image might make a beautiful scene for a Christmas greeting card, it does not help me sense God's love for me as an individual. Does God love the whole world only as a giant conglomeration of people, or does he know and *love me personally*? This is a classic example of knowing the words of God but not knowing the Word of God. The way I had pictured this Scripture verse since childhood, although perhaps majestic, was sterile and impersonal.

Since this mental picture wasn't helpful, I needed to develop another based on the truth of this passage. First, I read John 3:16 from *The Message*:

This is how much God loved the world: He gave his Son, his one and only Son. And this is why: so that no one need be destroyed; by believing in him, anyone can have a whole and lasting life.

I have found that to make this verse personal, I need to put myself in the picture. So when I read the first part of the verse, "This is how much God loved the world," I think, *This is how much God loved Jennifer . . .*

Then I try putting it in the first-person form, and I say, *This is how much God loved me . . .*

Then I actually say it out loud. "This is how much God loved me . . ."

And I don't just think it and say it quickly; I take several seconds or minutes to form a picture of what that really looks like—God loving me. I actually see a picture of a conversation between God the Father and myself. As I mentioned earlier, since God is spirit and no one has seen his face, I realize that my picture of him is imperfect; however, he has revealed his character in his Word and through Jesus, and our conversation reflects what he tells me about himself in the Bible.

As I think about this verse phrase by phrase, a complete picture forms in my mind. My heavenly Father is standing close to me, facing me and holding both of my hands in his. I take the meaning of John 3:16 and I put it into a statement addressed to me, face-to-face. With his eyes shining with adoring love, he tells me: "This is how much I love you, Jennifer. I gave my Son, my one and only Son. And this is why—so that you, Jennifer, don't need to be destroyed. By believing in him, you, Jennifer, can have a whole and lasting life. I didn't go to all the trouble of sending my Son merely to point an accusing finger, telling you, Jennifer, how bad you are. But I came to help put your world right again. And Jennifer, if you trust in me, you are acquitted."

When I first read this passage that way, tears welled up in my eyes, because the words reached out and grabbed me.

What great news! No matter what you've done in the past, no matter how unlovable you may feel, if you trust in the Lord, there is no judgment for you—only unconditional love. God gave his only Son so that you could experience this love—he is not standing up in heaven with his finger outstretched, waiting to strike you down as soon as you mess up. No—God's Word says that he did not send Jesus to condemn you, but to save you! What a difference!

When I grasped the significance of this concept, it revolutionized my life.

I began to realize that I didn't have to perform in order to win God's favor. I didn't *have* to lead five worship services a week to make him (or my family and friends) love me. I didn't have to be the perfect wife, mother, or daughter, living up to others' standards for me or my unrealistic standards for myself. I was lovable just the way I was.

This revelation must become real to you personally—it must sink itself deep down into your heart and penetrate your spirit before it will ever change your life. I am not telling you that you will never sin again, or that you will never make mistakes, but I am telling you that God loves you *in spite of* the things you do. You'll never reach perfection this side of heaven—nobody will. Each of us sins every day, but God's grace, through Jesus' blood, covers those sins, and his forgiveness is available to us when we repent of our behavior and ask him for a new chance, a fresh start.

The faithful love of the LORD never ends! . . . Great is his faithfulness; his mercies begin afresh each morning. (Lamentations 3:22-23)

The Holy Spirit spoke this truth to my heart one day when he said to me, *I love you, Jennifer. Yes, you do idiotic things sometimes—but I love you. And I forgive you!* What a relief it was to hear those words! I already knew that I make mistakes; no one has to remind me of that. But knowing that God loves me unconditionally, despite all of my sins, failures, and shortcomings, allowed me the freedom I needed to relax in his healing presence and soak in his love.

God's Word tells us that even before we came to him, *while we were still sinners*, he loved us enough to send his own Son to rescue us and bring us back to himself. To continue showing how to make his Word apply specifically to you, I'm going to personalize these verses. As you read these, please substitute your own name:

> Jennifer, when you were utterly helpless, I, Jesus Christ, came at just the right time and died for you, Jennifer, a sinner. Now, no one is likely to die for a good person, though someone might be willing to die for a person who is especially good. But God showed his great love for you, Jennifer, by sending me to die for you while you were still a sinner (just sitting there sick on your couch). And since you have been made right in God's sight by my blood, I will certainly save you from God's judgment. (See Romans 5:6-9.)

While I hear Christ explaining what he has done for me in the verses above, I use the next few verses to remind myself what Jesus' love means for me, both now and in the future:

For since I, Jennifer, was restored to friendship with God by the death of his Son while I was still his enemy, I will certainly be delivered from eternal punishment by his life. So now I can rejoice in my wonderful new relationship with God—all because of what our Lord Jesus Christ has done for me in making me a friend of God. (See vv. 10–11.)

We are God's friends! We are restored to a relationship with him and we have favor in his eyes. Not only that, but we are also adopted into his family, becoming his beloved children:

See how very much I, your heavenly Father, love you, for I allow you, Jennifer, to be called my daughter, and you really are! (See 1 John 3:1.)

[I am] God's very own child, adopted into his family—calling him "Father, dear Father." For his Holy Spirit speaks to me deep in my heart and tells me that I am God's child. (See Romans 8:15-16.)

Since I have become a parent myself, I have begun to understand the great love the Father has for his children.

There is nothing I wouldn't do for my kids—and God feels the same way about you and me! Don't believe the lie that would try to tell you that you are unlovable. On the contrary, you are immensely valuable, infinitely precious, and unfathomably loved.

MY PICTURE PRAYER EXPERIENCE

So far in this chapter, I've focused on the need I had to grasp the truth that God's love for me endured no matter where, when, or how often I fell short. Now I want to show you how I was able to hold on to the truth that God's love for others is also unconditional, even when because of their actions, they may seem unlovable.

As the wife of a pastor, I have had many opportunities throughout the years to see the ill behavior of people like myself that makes God's unconditional love seem stretched to the limits. One such situation involved a young woman I knew who had been betrayed by a young man. The hurtful actions seemed to irreparably damage both precious individuals. There was so much pain involved that even I myself, as one of their spiritual mentors, could hardly bear it. For days after I learned about the situation, I was extremely grieved. In my mind, I went back and forth between extreme anger and mournful pity as I played the circumstances over and over in my brain. I was desperately struggling as my thoughts were shouting these lies: *This situation is damaged beyond the ability to be healed. All is lost. This injury will be forever.* The anger I felt caused me to be tempted to believe the lie that one of these individuals was unlovable.

Because of the extreme negative emotions I was feeling, I supposed that I was processing something incorrectly. As I began to try to make sense of the truth of the situation, I decided to dwell on the truth by finding a truthful picture during my time of prayer. With the Holy Spirit's help, I began to form two pictures that brought me relief. I asked myself, *Where was God when this betrayal occurred?* I went through many images in my mind, but one that brought me peace and comfort was a picture of the two individuals in the midst of the awful circumstances of the betrayal. Surrounding them were angels in a protective circle all around. Instead of facing inside the circle watching, gawking, and accusing, the angels were facing out, shoulder to shoulder, as if they were protecting this couple from further injury.

I began to see that God had not been surprised or "off duty" at the time, but that he was actually ensuring that the situation, which could have been much worse, did not escalate further. This picture also helped me see God's love for all the individuals involved. Because of the value he placed on them, they warranted protection. That protection implied future hope, but I still needed something more concrete— something more redemptive in which to put my confidence.

What could be more redemptive than the cross?

But how could that wooden cross have any effect on this awful situation? I tried to picture where my loved ones stood in relation to the cross. All I could see was their brokenness, hurt, and pain. In my mind, they weren't even aware there was a cross. They were slumped, sitting down, leaning with their backs against the cross, barely able to raise their heads due to their despondency, guilt, and shame.

How could this sad picture help me?

I began to imagine Jesus hanging on the cross. The nails in his hands and feet and the wounds in his side were excruciatingly painful. He had every reason to feel sorry for himself or be preoccupied, but his thoughts were only on the unaware recipients below. As I watched, the blood flowed down from his body like a stream. The stream of blood began to cover my friends, beginning at the top of their heads and flowing all the way down their shoulders and bodies.

What happened next may seem strange, but it was a very powerful image. As the blood covered their faces, they began to relax and breathe deeply. Their bodies began to straighten and soften, and the expressions on their faces turned from ones of painful anguish to peaceful smiles. As the blood enveloped every cell of their bodies and covered every inch of their skin, they were washed clean and made new. The word that came to mind was *redeemed*.

I already knew this truth in the abstract, but to see this concrete picture of an abstract reality caused me to believe and trust. As this truth grabbed hold of me, I began to write some lyrics and put a melody to them. Later, when I shared the picture with my son, Chris, he was moved to complete the song with better melodies, chords, and lyrics.

He also wrote the powerful prayer in the first line of the chorus: "Blood, cover me—my everything! Come take over! Completely free—all of my life redeemed!"[3]

This powerful picture allowed me to see a spiritual truth in a way that helped me believe it. I didn't just have a fleeting, cognitive thought, *Yes, they are forgiven. What else is new?* The beautiful image that I dwelled on over and over throughout the next few weeks healed my hurt and pain. It allowed me to have compassion and forgiveness. It gave me hope because I saw an image not only of what *could be*, but what already *was* in God's eyes. My friends' lives were already redeemed! There was no hurt that God could not heal and no pain that love could not fight.

I pray that you will not fall prey to the Perfect Lie: *I must meet the standards others have set for me because otherwise I will be unlovable.* This is the truth: you are redeemed, made whole, and set free.

YOUR PICTURE PRAYER EXERCISE

Right now, take some time to sit quietly with your fingertips pressed together and try to find a picture in your mind of yourself being loved unconditionally. This could be an actual picture from your past in which you felt fully and completely loved, or it could be a picture of something you wish for, or it could be a picture of God loving you right where you are. If you'd like, take one of the following Statements or Scriptures to Ponder to help you form that truthful picture. If God were physically here with you now, what would he do for you, where you are *right now*, to show you how much he loves you? The truth is: he does love you! Develop this picture in detail and reflect on it for five minutes. Try taking time to bring to mind this same picture two more times today for five minutes at a time.

STATEMENTS TO PONDER

God loves me, and nothing in the universe can stop his love for me.

When I believe God, I can have a whole and lasting life.

God is not accusing me; he is not mad at me. He stands ready to forgive me when I make mistakes.

By accepting God's love for me, I give myself the power to become the kind of person I want to be.

SCRIPTURES TO PONDER

The LORD is compassionate and merciful,
    slow to get angry and filled with unfailing love. . . .
His unfailing love toward those who fear him
    is as great as the height of the heavens above the
        earth. (Psalm 103:8, 11)

We love Him because He first loved us. (1 John 4:19, NKJV)

Give thanks to the LORD, for he is good!
　　His faithful love endures forever. (Psalm 118:29)

CHAPTER 5

PERFECT LIE NUMBER TWO: I AM WORTHLESS

I MUST PROVE MYSELF BECAUSE MY WORTH
DEPENDS ON WHAT I DO.

It's my desire to see you, Lord.
In everything this life will bring
I want to find a way to spend
All I have for you, my King.

It may not seem like much
In light of all you made,
But it's all I have to give:
A life in love with you.

JENNIFER CROW, "LIFE IN LOVE," 2006

IN THE FALL OF 1993, my husband, Mark, felt God calling us to move our family and start a church in Oklahoma. At the time, he was the youth pastor and I was the worship leader at a church in Texas. I had begun to feel comfortable mentoring a bunch of teenagers, but now it appeared that

75

God was calling me out of my comfort zone once again. At least I would be in charge of planning music for our services, a role I enjoyed.

The first two people to join our church plant were Mark's cousin and his college friend, both of whom lived in the Oklahoma City area. Each of them told a few friends about our church, and before we knew it, a core group of people had committed themselves to the church start.

One of the couples, whom I'll call the Smiths, were my parents' age and were especially generous with their time, resources, and experience. In the months leading up to our first church service, Mark would drive up every four weeks from our home in Texas to hold a leaders' meeting. The Smiths offered to host those meetings in their home. They also helped Mark follow up on leads as he searched for a place to hold our worship services. When Mark wanted to introduce me to the leadership team, the Smiths invited our entire family to stay with them for a few days (quite a labor of love since our kids were eight, six, four, and two at the time).

At last, in August 1994, Victory Church held its first worship service. Fifty-three people came that morning, and the entire leadership team rejoiced to see how God was working in our small community. Of course, because we were such a small group and had no other church supporting us, everyone had to pitch in. I arrived early on Sundays for rehearsal and the sound check while other people set up the gymnasium and prepared the children's Sunday school area. Mark also began holding workdays on Saturdays, since we could not afford to hire a janitor or cleaning service. The two of us debated whether I should join him on those mornings; however, our four young children would have had to tag along, which probably would have resulted in a bigger mess! We decided it would be best for me to stay home with them.

During that first year, our church slowly began to grow and, more important, became a vibrant community as people who had first met as strangers bonded together in their love for Christ and commitment to Victory Church. Then one day Mark came home and dropped a bombshell: the Smiths had decided to leave our congregation.

I was certain there must be a misunderstanding, so I called Mrs. Smith to find out what had happened. She began listing numerous ways in which Mark and I had let her and her husband down. There seemed to be a common thread to her concerns: Mark and I were not being as "hands on" as they thought we needed to be. As examples, she pointed out that I never came to the Saturday workdays or helped out in the nursery, which she attributed to my feeling that such duties were beneath me.

I was crushed. I wanted to ask her, "Can't you see why it doesn't make sense for me to come on Saturday mornings? How could I serve in the nursery when I need to arrive an hour early for rehearsal and participate in the worship time?" I was so stunned, though, that I didn't say much of anything. I had been trying so hard to prove my worth as a pastor's wife. And now because of what I wasn't able to do, one of our key families had left the church. I cried for three days and agonized over what I should have done differently. I felt worthless and like a failure. Maybe I just wasn't cut out for ministry.

It may seem at times that God doesn't know what he is doing when he calls us to do things for him. You and I may look back upon all our failures and wonder whether God can really use us. We may be easily discouraged by others' criticism. A sharp word or even a disapproving look can leave us feeling hurt or insulted.

Sometimes we doubt our worth not because of others' negative reactions to us, but because we feel we aren't accomplishing enough. After all, our culture puts a high premium on achievement. I can certainly relate to that trap as well. For the first four years after I married Mark, I worked full-time programming digital phone systems and selling the systems to large companies. I earned a commission based on what I sold, and those checks reflected my worth to the company.

I went through quite an adjustment after I had my first two children within eighteen months of one another. Rather than being affirmed for what I did, I was suddenly being ignored for what I did. No one gave me a bonus for setting a record for the number of diapers changed in a day or the number of times I comforted a crying child.

I have always loved my children dearly, but during those early days as a mom, I remember wondering, *What is my worth? What is my value, now that it can't be measured?* The Bible says that children are a blessing from the Lord, but our culture and media do not always promote that message. In fact, they often portray children as a burden. As a result, sometimes young moms get the idea that their contribution of love and care is not worthy of respect, honor, or admiration.

If you often doubt your worth, either because of a past failure or your present circumstances, you may resonate with the second Perfect Lie:

> *I must prove myself*
> *because my worth depends on what I do.*

Failure is inevitable at some point in everyone's life, but thank God, our worth is not determined by our performance. It is determined by the great love our heavenly Father has lavished upon us. He loved us so much that he sent his only Son to die on the cross to save us!

Maybe you intellectually know and understand God's love for you, yet you still experience feelings of worthlessness and its partner, hopelessness. Such feelings make you more likely to pay attention to self-accusations like the following (especially when you feel you have "messed up"):

You'll never amount to anything.
You are so uncoordinated!
You are so clumsy.

You are so stupid!
Your situation is completely hopeless.

During the recent "Great Recession" and its aftermath, an untold number of Americans have been forced to rethink the source of their worth. One news reporter interviewed fifty-three-year-old J. R. Childress about how long-term unemployment was affecting him. The former construction executive began working immediately after high school and eventually earned a six-figure salary as a vice president of operations. Laid off from that position in the fall of 2009, Childress finally landed a new position as a construction foreman over a year later. Even though he took a huge pay cut, Childress was grateful to be employed again. Several months later, however, that job also ended. Today he struggles to keep busy but is open about his struggles to find self-worth. Long-term unemployment, he says, "makes you feel you're not a part of society because you're not earning your way."[4] One psychologist, speaking of those who have been laid off from work, comments, "You can have all kinds of people like spouses and friends say you are terrific . . . but in the core, you say, I am not, and I have big evidence that I am not. Layoffs . . . literally deplete life."[5]

Of course, feelings of worthlessness can also stem from a divorce, a blowup with a rebellious teenage child, or even retirement. Regardless of its source, when we find our value in anything other than the immense worth God puts on us, we will experience some of the following emotions:

Emotions associated with this lie

~ *sadness*

~ *depression*

~ *inferiority*

Amazingly, we have a Savior who knows what it feels like to be overlooked and disregarded. Over seven hundred years before the Messiah's birth, the prophet Isaiah described how he would be received: "There was nothing beautiful or majestic about his appearance, nothing to attract us to him. He was despised and rejected—a man of sorrows, acquainted with deepest grief. We turned our backs on him and looked the other way. He was despised, and we did not care" (Isaiah 53:2-3). Jesus, the Creator of the universe, willingly set aside his exalted position to come to earth and pay the debt we owed but could never repay. Instead of glorifying him, many of his chosen people rejected him. And many people still reject him today. As Oswald Chambers once wrote, "Sum up the life of Jesus by any other standard than God's, and it is an anticlimax of failure."

And that's the point: neither Jesus nor his Father saw his life on earth that way. The Messiah's worth was not based on how well he was accepted by men or by any standard of human achievement. And on the night before he was killed, Jesus was able to rest in his Father's love, telling his disciples: "I have loved you even as the Father has loved me. Remain in my love" (John 15:9).

Jesus was beloved by his Father, and you are of great worth to him as well!

LIE DETECTOR TEST

Perhaps you don't really believe God truly loves you. Ask yourself the following questions to determine if you believe the Perfect Lie: *I must prove myself because my worth depends on what I do.*

- Does it seem as if the things you do never turn out the way you expected?
- Have you experienced repeated failures? Dropped out of school? Been divorced? Been fired from a job? Started a business that failed?
- How easily can you let go of past failures and move on to something new?
- Do you consider the work you do as a stay-at-home mom [or student or retired person or caretaker] as not very significant?

Some Christians assume the Bible promises them that they will never suffer or face problems. But Scripture is clear that we will experience trouble. Sometimes the trouble may be caused by us, but sometimes it is completely outside of our control. And let's face it: you and I have blown it. You *may* have been divorced once, or more than once. It might even have been "your fault." Your current marriage may be heading in the wrong direction. Your children might be in trouble. In the midst of such challenges, one of the most debilitating lies is that you are worthless. After all, such a mind-set leads you to tell yourself, *I am worth nothing, so what's the point? What hope do I have for a better future?*

In the midst of every adversity that you face, *you* have the power to stand up and address the lying thoughts that invade your mind by reinforcing the truth: "I am not worthless. My life is not hopeless. And, with God's help, I will work to turn this around for my good, for the good of those around me, and for the good of the world in which I live."

That *is* the gospel, pure and simple: God loves you just the way you are.

ANTIDOTE TO THE SECOND PERFECT LIE

What truth will help us counteract the second lie, *I must prove myself because my worth depends on what I do*?

I like to keep things simple.

What could be simpler than Psalm 23, one of the best-known Bible passages in history? It's likely you are already familiar with this passage. I want to show you how to take what you may already know and apply it personally so you can begin to change your thoughts.

As I recovered from my own breakdown, I meditated on this Scripture nearly every day, especially at night when negative thoughts of failure or worthlessness prevented me from sleeping. When I meditate on Psalm 23, I don't just quote it; I purposefully create a movie script of it in my head. When I learned this Scripture as a child in Sunday school, I pictured cute little fluffy baby lambs being cared for by Jesus, the shepherd with a shepherd's crook. It's a pretty picture, but it doesn't generate the personal power that comes when I put myself into the story.

I know that this Scripture is personifying Jesus as a shepherd and the writer as a sheep, but when I visualize this, I don't see myself as a sheep, because, well—I just can't relate to that . . . *baaaaa!* I see myself as me, a human, walking with Jesus, whose job is to care for, protect, and guide me. As I envision this, my body responds physiologically to the happy and peaceful thoughts this passage creates, and I build new, truth-based neuropathways in my brain. This time, I want to take the psalm phrase by phrase:

The LORD is my shepherd . . .
Sometimes when I am meditating on a Scripture, I emphasize different words to help make the meaning real. The *Lord* is your shepherd. How amazing to consider that the Creator of the universe is your personal guide, teacher, and provider. The *Lord* is *your* shepherd. The Lord, not your husband, not your mama, not your best friend, takes care of you and guides you in the right way. That's how much he loves you; that's how much worth and hope you have. The *Lord*, Creator of heaven and earth, is *your* shepherd.

I shall not want . . .
If you don't want anything, that means you are not lacking anything. If you ever do lack something, God will

provide. There's nothing you need that God will not give you. Would God make sure you had everything you needed if you were worthless? No! You shall not want because he is your shepherd.

There is nothing that God cannot give you, nothing that he will not provide for your life. There is *always* hope in *every* situation!

He makes me to lie down in green pastures . . .
If you have ever cared for a baby or toddler, you know that most kids fight taking their naps. But when her little one starts getting cranky, Mama knows it is time for her child to rest. In the same way, God "makes" you and me lie down and get our rest. Notice that God is not forcing us to lie down in a field of dirt or mud either. We are worth far more than that to him. He allows us to rest in the *green* pastures of his presence and love.

He leads me beside still waters . . .
Those still waters represent the inner peace you can have in spite of adversity around you. Each day God, within your thoughts and spirit, leads you beside quiet waters. Not rapids that are going to rock your boat. Not waterfalls in which you'll drown. Not tidal waves that will bowl you over. You may still face challenges, but you are of such worth to God that he will enable you to walk in perfect inner peace as you learn to direct your thoughts toward him.

He restores my soul . . .

The soul is the very innermost part of you from which all of your emotions emanate. And your emotions impact every area of your life—your walk with God, your relationships with others, and your physical health. Your soul is the innermost part of your being. When you are feeling like you are soulless, wrung out, and worn down with nothing left, you can picture God touching you and restoring your soul. His love has the power to heal your soul and make it whole once again.

As you meditate on any of these phrases, *The LORD is my shepherd . . . I shall not want . . . He makes me to lie down in green pastures . . . He leads me beside still waters . . . He restores my soul,* picture the Lord tenderly caring for you in that way. Remind yourself, my soul is worth tending and restoring. I have value. I'm not worthless, and I'm not hopeless.

I encourage you to meditate on the other verses in Psalm 23 as well. As you do, notice that whether our Lord is protecting you, correcting you, or blessing you, his love and concern stem from the value he places on you, not on anything you have done.

You matter to God! Just consider how David ends his psalm: "Surely goodness and mercy shall follow me all the days of my life; and I will dwell in the house of the LORD forever."

Earlier in this chapter, I mentioned how I struggled with self-worth following the birth of our children. During much of that time, Mark traveled and preached at different churches as an itinerant minister. By then we had four children under the age of five, so I rarely was able to go with him.

However, on one occasion our family was able to stay with friends as Mark preached in California. The pastor at one of the churches where Mark was scheduled to speak asked me to sing before he gave his message. It was the first time in quite a while that I'd been able to sing publicly, and the audience seemed to enjoy it.

The pastor liked the singing so much that he told the friend we were staying with that I should do more of it. When my friend explained that I was too busy caring for our small children, the pastor said something that I have never forgotten: "Having Jennifer Crow taking care of all those kids is like tying up a racehorse to a plowshare!"

He meant his words as a compliment, but I wondered if I was wasting my gifts and talents because I had to focus my energy on raising my children rather than on a music career or ministry.

I felt I heard God's voice in my heart asking, *Jennifer, if you had been the only human being on earth who had been imprisoned by sin, wouldn't I have sent my Son, Jesus Christ, to die on the cross just for you? If only your life was at stake, wouldn't it have been worth it to give my life for yours?* In fact, I *did* know that God loved me so much that he would have died just for me, even if I had been the only one who needed that sacrifice.

I felt God ask, *Then why wouldn't I send my "great" Jennifer*

Crow just to love and care for Christopher, Evangelyn, Andrew, and Joseph? Are they not worth it?

As their mom, I can say without reservation that they are invaluable to me! Worth is measured by how much value is placed on a person or object by the one who loves it. Our worth is based on how much we are loved by God and how much he wants to spend eternity with us. He gave up the life of his own Son, God in the flesh, to save us. Our worth is not based on what we do, but on how much we are loved.

MY PICTURE PRAYER EXPERIENCE

When I was about four years old, my mother had what they called in those days a "nervous breakdown." At only twenty-six, she was unable to care for me and my little brother and had to stay in bed for days at a time. She had issues of her own from the past with her parents, and she was dealing with the typical pressures that most moms face: financial, marital, and parental. I'm guessing she felt overwhelmed by her life.

When she was bedridden, she would keep the shades and curtains drawn during the middle of the day. She kept a little brass bell at her bedside, and when she needed something, she would ring the bell and my dad would come and help her. Her illness left me frightened. It also made me feel responsible to find some way to make her feel better.

I have a vivid memory that sticks with me even now: One sunny day, I decided to go into the backyard and pick some wildflowers that I could bring to my mom to cheer her up.

I now know that those "beautiful wildflowers" were actually weeds that had grown up in the South Texas springtime because my dad had not been able to mow the yard. It was everything he could do just to work and take care of his kids since Mom was sick.

Nevertheless, I went out all alone and pulled up a fistful of squashed and wilted flowers, an offering of hope from my heart. I went back into the house and walked to the dark threshold of my mother's bedroom door. I felt as if I were facing the very darkness of hell itself. I was holding my light, my hope, to make my mother feel better—but I knew it was nothing compared to the darkness coming from that stifling room.

I don't remember what happened after that, but the picture of me as a scared, helpless preschooler trying to stand against the darkness was burned into my memory for a lifetime. Even after forty years, that picture in my mind could still put a chill into my soul. Somehow, I felt, I was to blame for my mom's continued illness—I couldn't make things right. I couldn't do what needed to be done. My contribution was worthless.

One day during my own illness when I was learning to change the pictures in my heart, this memory came back to me. By then, I had begun to try to identify each lie that had a hold on my life by considering what emotion was associated with it. I'd ask myself, *When is the first time you can remember experiencing this emotion?* One day I asked myself my earliest memory of feeling worthless and hopeless. That is how I unearthed this picture.

I began to ask myself, *What is the truth about this picture? What lie am I believing?* I had been experiencing the memory through the understanding of a four-year-old child, but what, in truth, was really happening there?

After experimenting with different scenarios in my mind's eye, here is the new picture that now replaces that dark scene: When I step to the threshold, Jesus meets me at the door, drops to his knees with a huge smile, and puts his arm around me as if he has been waiting for me all day. He tenderly and cheerfully says, "Hi, Jen! What's going on?"

He follows my tentative stare toward my mother's bedside, and then says, "Look, Jennifer. See—you don't have to be afraid . . ."

As I follow his gesture, I can see the Holy Spirit close at my mother's side, bending over her and stroking her arms and hair. Even though her pained expression shows that she is completely unaware of his presence, he is caring for her and ministering to her every need.

Jesus turns to me and says, "Don't worry about her, Jennifer. We are taking good care of her. Now, let's go outside and play!"

This picture makes me smile. This picture gives me peace. When I first saw this picture in my heart, the peace of God began to fill my body as my tension relaxed. As I began to reflect on this new picture during my prayer time for the next few days, the power and reality of the new picture overtook the fear associated with the old picture. Now, even today, when I think of that incident, I experience a feeling of joy and fulfillment, knowing that God loves me. My worth is not dependent on someone else's pain or happiness. I do not have to prove my worth by what I do or by measuring up to a standard. God is taking care of me and those whom I love. I don't have to feel worthless and hopeless anymore.

YOUR PICTURE PRAYER EXERCISE

When you were a child, what gave you the greatest feelings of affirmation? Was it getting a gold star or an A+ in school? Was it hearing the voice of a parent saying, "I'm so proud of you"? How might you receive those same feelings of affirmation from the Lord today?

In the Bible, Jesus washed the feet of his disciples on the night before his crucifixion to show his love and affirmation for them. For me, picturing Jesus washing my hair allows me to experience the immense worth I have in his eyes. What picture of Jesus most reminds you of your own worth to him? Remember—you are so valuable to the Father that even if you had been the only person on the earth, he still would have sent his Son to die—for you!

STATEMENTS TO PONDER

My worth is not determined by my beauty, by my achievements, by my possessions, or by my financial status. Jesus

Christ showed me my true value when he gave himself on the cross—for me.

My life counts! I am God's precious child!

My past does not define my future. I am free to live in the present, mindful of my value to God.

I am not worthless—I am more valuable than I could ever imagine because of the love that the Father has poured into my life.

SCRIPTURES TO PONDER

GOD, my shepherd!
    I don't need a thing.
You have bedded me down in lush meadows,
    you find me quiet pools to drink from.

True to your word,
    you let me catch my breath
    and send me in the right direction.

Even when the way goes through
    Death Valley,
I'm not afraid
    when you walk at my side.
Your trusty shepherd's crook
    makes me feel secure.

You serve me a six-course dinner
 right in front of my enemies.
You revive my drooping head;
 my cup brims with blessing.

Your beauty and love chase after me
 every day of my life.
I'm back home in the house of GOD
 for the rest of my life. (Psalm 23, THE MESSAGE)

How precious are your thoughts about me, O God.
 They cannot be numbered!
I can't even count them;
 they outnumber the grains of sand!
  (Psalm 139:17-18)

What shall we say about such wonderful things as these? If God is for us, who can ever be against us? Since he did not spare even his own Son but gave him up for us all, won't he also give us everything else? . . .

I am convinced that nothing can ever separate us from God's love. Neither death nor life, neither angels nor demons, neither our fears for today nor our worries about tomorrow—not even the powers of hell can separate us from God's love. No power in the sky above or in the earth below—indeed, nothing in all creation will ever be able to separate us

from the love of God that is revealed in Christ Jesus
our Lord. (Romans 8:31-32, 38-39)

CHAPTER 6

PERFECT LIE NUMBER THREE: I AM UNACCEPTABLE

I MUST GAIN THE ACCEPTANCE OF OTHERS
BECAUSE THEIR OPINION MATTERS MOST.

How can I know the depth of love
That made the world and the stars above?
What can explain this love I feel?
In darkest days I know you're real.
How I remember your love for me.
Your dying breath surely set me free.

Hallelujah, rejoice, my soul!
You're unfailing love, forever.
My deliverer, my strength, my rock,
Your great faithfulness, I remember.

CHRIS CROW AND JENNIFER CROW,
"HYMN OF REMEMBRANCE," 2010

WHILE IN THE African country of Lesotho recently, I went
shopping for housewares that would be used by a shelter
for victims of human trafficking. I went to the brand-new

Pioneer Mall, the first such shopping center in the entire country.

As I stood in line at one store to buy some dishes, my eyes were drawn to a toy display near the checkout counter. It was filled with beautiful baby dolls in various outfits. There were blond-haired, blue-eyed dolls; brown-haired, green-eyed dolls; black-haired, brown-eyed dolls; and even some red-haired dolls (well . . . bright-orange hair, let's say). There seemed to be every kind of white-skinned doll, but my heart sank as I looked at row after row without seeing a single brown-skinned doll. How could this be in a country where 99.7 percent of the population belongs to the African Basotho tribe?

I tried to imagine the cause of this bias. Was there not a supply of brown-skinned dolls available to this store? Did the store's owner purchase only white-skinned dolls because they sold best? No matter the reason, I thought how invalidating it must feel to Basotho girls who never find a doll that looks like them.

This is an example of the type of degrading subliminal message that has long been sent to an entire race of children. *I am not acceptable based on the color of my skin.* Such a ridiculous lie, yet it seems humans have always used arbitrary measuring sticks like appearance, language, dress, poverty, and religious beliefs to determine whether other people are acceptable.

Yet sometimes this rejection occurs on a smaller scale, as when parents abandon their child or favor one child over another. In 2011, Americans were horrified to learn that a father and stepmother had kept their thirteen-year-old son, Christian, locked in a three-foot-high dog cage, telling their other children, "He needs to be locked up. He's a dog." On a piece of paper no one outside his family saw until after his death, he wrote, "I want to die." He also wrote about his anguish as he wondered why no one in his family loved him. Eventually, Christian was beaten to death.[6]

Obviously, this is an extreme example of horrific abuse. Yet any child who feels rejected from an early age must live with the scars forever. One of Eleanor Roosevelt's earliest memories, for instance, is of hearing her beautiful mother, Anna, describe her this way: "She is such a funny child, so old-fashioned that we always call her Granny." Clearly disappointed in her daughter's plain looks, Anna tried to instill impeccable manners in her firstborn child to make up for her "deficiency." Sadly, Anna died just a few years later, so Eleanor never felt truly accepted by her.[7]

Some sins, such as racism, are systemic evils that affect an entire group of people. Family sins like neglect, abuse, and abandonment may cripple their victims permanently. And many other people battle loneliness and fear because they are bullied by their classmates, coworkers, and neighbors.

Perhaps you have always been told, directly or indirectly, that you are undesirable or unwanted. If so, no matter how good you look on the outside or how well you perform, you are one of countless people who must constantly battle this lie:

> *I must gain the acceptance of others
> because their opinion matters most.*

The messages you hear in your head are very likely the same messages you heard from the mouths of family members or peers:

> *There is something wrong with you.*
> *You are ugly.*
> *You are dumb.*
> *You aren't as important as your sibling.*

As a child, I loved Dr. Seuss books, and when I had my own kids, I used them to teach my children to read. One of our favorites was *The Sneetches*. In the story, these interesting-looking creatures called the Sneetches all look very similar—except that some have a star on their bellies and some do not. For some reason, this star or lack of a star determines a Sneetch's social status. Sometimes it is cool to have a star; at other times it is not. An enterprising stranger takes advantage of the Sneetches' obsession over this feature and invents a machine that can put on or take off stars, depending on what is in fashion. He makes a fortune before the Sneetches realize just how silly they have been. Star or no star, they are all the same inside. The reason this story is so powerful, of course, is that it mirrors how we human beings act toward one another.

Every one of us looks to our culture, our community, and our parents to help us determine whether we measure up.

When we are told we've fallen short, we're likely to feel some of these emotions:

Emotions associated with this lie
- *insecurity*
- *shame*
- *false pride (when we do achieve some degree of "perfection" in our own eyes)*

Something as silly as our hair type can make us feel alienated. I was born with thick, curly hair. That was great in the eighties when everyone was getting perms, crimps, curls, and three-inch-high bangs. But before that, when I was approaching adolescence in the midseventies, it was impossible for me to achieve the "in" hairstyle: long and straight, parted in the middle.

Oh, how I wanted that hairstyle! I tried everything to get that look, from rolling my wet hair on empty frozen-orange-juice cans to having a friend iron it on the ironing board. (This was before the days of flat irons and blow-dryers.) But since I lived in hot and humid South Texas, five minutes after straightening my hair, it was a frizzy mess once again.

All my friends had long, straight, beautiful hair! Why couldn't I? I cried and lost sleep and boyfriends (in my imagination), all because I believed a lie that said that I was unacceptable because of the way I looked. What drove my obsession to look like Peggy Lipton on *The Mod Squad* anyway? Peer pressure. I wanted to live up to what everyone around me considered "cool."

If you believe this lie, you too may be preoccupied with what others think about you, and most likely, that preoccupation controls much of your behavior. I know, because this was a lie that dictated almost every minute of every day for the first forty-three years of my life.

LIE DETECTOR TEST

Ask yourself the following questions to determine if you believe the Perfect Lie: *I must gain the acceptance of others because their opinion matters most.*

- Do you ever feel as if you are not as "good" as the people around you?

- Do you constantly feel a sense of rejection, even among people you consider friends?

- Do you ever feel unworthy of God's love?

- Have you ever said or done anything that you think is so horrific that no one—including God—could ever love you again?

When we allow ourselves to be influenced by this lie, we find ourselves trying to keep everyone happy to avoid conflict. We may have a charming personality and even be the life of the party, but this ugly lie keeps simmering in the back of our mind: *I have to keep up this façade. I have to make sure everybody loves me. I hope nothing happens that shows people the real me.*

We may also feel compelled to appear perfect to other people. That way, they will have no reason to reject us. Really? Let's remember again the only man who was ever perfect in this life: Jesus Christ. Could he have been more loving? No. Could he have been a better leader? No. Could he have handled the negative situations in his life any better? No. And yet he was murdered. His perfect behavior did not keep people from rejecting him just as our "perfect" behavior will not keep people from rejecting us. His enemies nailed him to the cross!

In the last chapter, we looked at Isaiah 53:2-3 to see how little worth the Jewish leaders and their followers put on Jesus, the Messiah. Verse 4 gives us an even more stunning look at how they viewed Jesus: "It was our weaknesses he carried; it was our sorrows that weighed him down. And we thought his troubles were a punishment from God, a punishment for his own sins!"

Amazing! Jesus, the perfect Lamb of God, was utterly rejected. If he, being without fault, experienced this persecution, then how much more must we realize that we are fighting a losing battle when we try to gain acceptance from others based on social standards. He understands what it feels like to be considered unacceptable.

ANTIDOTE TO THE THIRD PERFECT LIE

I like to use the simplest, best-known Scriptures to show the power of God's truth to change a lie. Many people have heard the story of Zacchaeus in the Bible. Even if they don't regularly attend church, they may have heard the children's song "Zacchaeus Was a Wee Little Man" when they visited vacation Bible school or a Sunday school class.

Remember some of the details of Luke's account in chapter 19? A chief tax collector named Zacchaeus heard that Jesus would be coming through town. He wanted to get a good look at this teacher, but he was too short to see over the crowd—and too despised to get a front-row seat. He worked as a tax collector for the Romans, so his fellow Jews considered him a traitor, and they hated him even more because he regularly cheated them.

Yet something was happening inside Zacchaeus's heart, and he refused to let the people's rejection keep him from seeing Jesus. He climbed a sycamore tree along the route Jesus would be taking through Jericho.

Something was drawing this rich little man to Christ, which explains his reaction when Jesus spotted him in the tree: "When Jesus came by, he looked up at Zacchaeus and called him by name. 'Zacchaeus!' he said. 'Quick, come down! I must be a guest in your home today.' Zacchaeus quickly climbed down and took Jesus to his house in great excitement and joy" (Luke 19:5-6).

No doubt Jesus knew all about this little man's past. He

certainly wasn't in favor of anyone stealing from someone else, as Zacchaeus had done. And yet, Jesus accepted him before he repented without the condition of repentance and asked to go to his house and eat with him.

What a picture of radical love! And what's true for Zacchaeus is true for us—God knows about all of our faults and failures and yet is willing to take us as we are. No matter what our parents, our culture, or our peers say about us, "Christ has accepted you" (Romans 15:7).

If there was any question as to how his neighbors felt about Zacchaeus, that was quickly settled. Displeased, they grumbled about Jesus' plans to be the guest "of a notorious sinner" (Luke 19:7). They had clearly written off the tax collector.

Imagine how suspicious the townspeople must have been later on when they heard Zacchaeus promise to give half his wealth away and repay all those he had cheated. Jesus, however, was delighted: "Salvation has come to this home today, for this man has shown himself to be a true son of Abraham. For the Son of Man came to seek and save those who are lost" (Luke 19:9-10).

This story proves that Jesus does not view us through the eyes of what society says is or isn't acceptable. He's willing to be with us, even risking that we might not end up choosing his love. One of my favorite quotes is by my friend and Christian speaker Sy Rogers, who expresses God's unconditional acceptance toward us this way: "I'd rather have you messy than not have you at all."

As you take a moment to meditate on this familiar Scripture passage, I encourage you to replace your image of Zacchaeus, the wee little man in the tree, with an image of yourself. I want you to picture yourself up in that tree hiding, perhaps cloaked in robes or other clothing to hide what's underneath—the "real" you that seems unacceptable to society or your family.

Everyone you see below, on the ground with Jesus, seems to be acceptable, a part of the "in" crowd, the "happy club." Up in that tree you feel isolated and alone—different and unacceptable. When you first see Jesus coming down the road, he doesn't seem to notice you. It seems likely that he will pass right by without ever noticing you, which is fine with you because you know you don't fit in and wouldn't be expecting to hang with the "big dogs."

But then you are startled when Jesus looks up as he walks by, smiling as if he had been looking for you all the time. He stops and says your name: "Hi! What are you doing up there? I was missing you, girl! Come on down, because I want to come over to your place for lunch today!" He stops and waits as you awkwardly but excitedly climb down the tree. Then he grabs you, gives you a big affectionate hug, and puts his arm around you, his special friend, as you both continue walking with the crowd toward your house.

He has singled you out! He knows your issues. He knows what you've done and what you go through on a daily basis, and yet he wants to have lunch with *you*! Your sin, faults, and failures do not scare him. He is not annoyed or disturbed or surprised by anything he sees in you—and he *does* see it all! He is not ashamed to be seen with you and would even give you special treatment in front of others. You are a part of his team, his family.

He accepts you radically.

As you let this truth sink in, remember that you and I can take our eyes off the people around us and stop looking for acceptance from anyone other than Jesus. Place your eyes on the One who values you, regardless of what others think—the One who died for you. Keep focusing on that picture of him calling you down from that tree and walking with you through the crowd. Realize that you are accepted!

If you ever doubt his unqualified love for you, just look at Romans 8:38: "I am convinced that nothing can ever separate us from God's love." If nothing can separate you from God's love, then you don't have to be a certain way to be okay. You are already okay because he already loves you.

The fear of rejection that you may be experiencing—as real as it may *seem*—can't separate you from his love. Even your worries and insecurities can't separate you from the love of God that you find in Jesus Christ.

It doesn't matter what the rest of the world thinks, says, or does: If God is for you, who can be against you?

MY PICTURE PRAYER EXPERIENCE

When I was battling the multiple physical conditions that seemed to have taken over my body, I lost a lot of my long, thick, curly hair because of extreme hormonal imbalances. It seemed to come out in fistfuls in the shower, in the tub, and at the vanity where I would dry and fix my hair—it was everywhere! I tried to keep it cleaned up, but there always seemed to be strands of my hair in our bathroom.

My husband is very neat and particular. He likes things just so. He has always done an excellent job of helping to keep our household orderly and on schedule. He also likes to have his private space. On the contrary, as a mom of five children spaced closely together, I had no personal space for years. Kids were constantly borrowing things from our bathroom, using our bathroom, and barging in to talk to me when I was getting ready in our bathroom. I was accustomed to living as one big, happy commune where everything was community property, but Mark thought of bathroom space and bathroom time more like a sacred retreat.

So when my strands of hair started appearing all over our bathroom, he sometimes got after me to clean them up. One day when he commented on it (without any intention of being unkind), I felt very hurt. I felt like he was disgusted by me and that he was uncompassionate toward my situation. I began to feel that familiar pressure to try gaining his acceptance because I felt I couldn't live without knowing he had a good opinion of me.

At this point, I had just started learning how to reprogram my thoughts, so I took a few minutes for meditative prayer later that day. I began this time by asking myself, *What am*

I feeling right now? and *What is bothering me right now?* The memory of Mark's disappointment over finding my hair all over the bathroom came to my mind. I had learned that all thoughts are stored as pictures, and if there was a hurtful picture in my mind, I was beginning to learn to heal it by changing it to a truthful picture.

I asked myself, *What is the truth about all of this hair you are losing? Mark doesn't really want to be around it or touch it, but what is really true about this situation?*

I began to wonder how Jesus would respond to my hair. I imagined him in the room with me, reaching down as he spotted a long, dark strand of my curly hair.

I imagined him holding it up to the light and saying, "Look at this beautiful hair! I made it, Jennifer, and I know about every strand of hair on your head. In fact, I have counted every one. Not one strand of hair falls off your head that I do not know about. This hair is an amazing part of my beautiful creation. Don't ever be ashamed of this hair, no matter what the situation. I am never ashamed of it, and I am never ashamed of you, my beautiful daughter."

During my time of meditative prayer that day, tears of joy and relief began to flow. At the darkest period of my life—when I couldn't even keep my body from betraying me and when my loving husband couldn't mask his frustration—these beautiful pictures of God's love filled my heart and began reprogramming my mind. My body was relaxing and being healed.

YOUR PICTURE PRAYER EXERCISE

Think of a recent time when you felt stressed about measuring up to someone's expectations. Were you truly unacceptable, or were you believing a lie? Now think of the first time in your life that you can ever remember feeling that way. Take some time to identify the picture associated with that memory, and use your knowledge of God's acceptance of you to change the picture in your mind to reflect the truth.

STATEMENTS TO PONDER

I will always find some people who are better than me and some who are worse. God loves me just the way I am.

I do not have to have the right things to be worthy of love.

My behavior is not what causes God to love me. He loves me because I am me, created in his image.

I don't have to compare myself to others to feel good about myself.

SCRIPTURES TO PONDER

Christ has accepted you. (Romans 15:7)

I am convinced that nothing can ever separate us from God's love. Neither death nor life, neither angels nor demons, neither our fears for today nor our worries about tomorrow—not even the powers of hell can separate us from God's love. No power in the sky above or in the earth below—indeed, nothing in all creation will ever be able to separate us from the love of God that is revealed in Christ Jesus our Lord. (Romans 8:38-39)

CHAPTER 7

PERFECT LIE NUMBER FOUR: I AM UNABLE

I MUST PULL BACK
BECAUSE I AM LESS CAPABLE THAN OTHERS.

I have all your love.
You've poured it out on me.
All you are in all your power
Is more than all I need.

I will rise with you.
You've set my spirit free.
I will live to give you praise
For all eternity.

JENNIFER CROW, JARON NIX, AND KRISTY STARLING,
"RISE," 2006

ONE NIGHT IN MARCH 2008, I had the most unusual dream of my life.

In my dream, my friend Christine and I were on what seemed like a tour boat traveling through the ocean. We were standing toward the front of the boat, looking over the railing across the water toward a rocky shore. At one point we

111

passed a large group of black seals, what seemed like hundreds or thousands of them, huddled together among the rocks along the coast. In the sky above, I saw a strange word spelled in capital letters: L E S O T H O. I was puzzled, never having heard or seen this word before.

As I looked back at the seals, I saw a large mother seal, two or three times bigger than the other seals, lying in the center of the group. She had a pouch like a kangaroo's, and in that pouch were hundreds of baby seals in different stages of development. Some were embryos and some were tiny seals; some were red and bloody; some were whitish or gray, as if ill; and some were black. As our boat passed by, Christine and I watched helplessly as we saw the mother seal's pouch tear and all the baby seals spill into the water, where they were lost.

As we looked into the face of the mother seal, her face turned into the face of a plain yet beautiful woman with smooth, medium-brown skin. Her large brown eyes met ours as tears slowly trickled down her cheeks. As she looked at us mournfully, she didn't have to say a word. Her eyes said it all . . . "Help me."

That was the end of my dream.

When I woke, I told Mark about the dream. He told me he had no idea what Lesotho meant either. Just for fun, I used Google to search for "Lesotho seals" and was shocked to learn that Lesotho is actually a country in southern Africa, which is surrounded on all sides by South Africa. I discovered a sixty-page report on human trafficking from the United

Nations, which said that Lesotho had the third highest HIV/AIDS infection rate per capita in the world.

I didn't even know Lesotho was a word, much less a country! As I processed this information, one of my first thoughts sounded a lot like the fourth Perfect Lie: *Why is this woman from Africa asking me to help her? I can't do anything! I'm only a pastor's wife halfway across the world in Oklahoma. I'm a mom of five children. I'm not a world traveler like my husband is. I'm not able to do anything to help.*

I tried to put off the responsibility of my dream on several other people, including my husband and Christine. I suggested Mark go to Lesotho to teach a leadership class. I asked Christine if she and her husband, Nick, might want to start a human trafficking rescue shelter in Lesotho as they had done in Greece. Neither Mark nor Christine felt God calling them to do what I'd suggested!

I know how tempting it is to shrink before an obstacle, focusing on our own inabilities and weaknesses, which inevitably leads to thoughts like these:

I can't do it; I'm not capable.
Everything I touch, I mess up.
I'm disabled; how could I possibly help?
I'm poor; I'll always have to struggle to make ends meet and will never have anything to offer other people.

For many of us, these ideas have been ingrained in us since childhood. A parent or teacher we loved or respected may have told us we were unable to do something, or that life would always be difficult for us, and we believed them. If so, we are vulnerable to the Perfect Lie:

I must pull back because I am less capable than others.

For much of my life, this lie—that I was "not able"—was one of the most tempting for me to believe. I refused to believe I was capable and qualified to do *anything* God called me to do. Every time God would ask me to do something new, I would dig in my heels and think with a whiny voice, *God, it's too hard! Get somebody else. Lord, I cannot do this. Call someone else, someone who's better than me.*

I'm dating myself here, but back when Evie and Sandi Patty were two of the most popular Christian singers, I would constantly compare my talents with theirs and complain to the Lord: *There are tons of better singers than me, God. If I can't sing like Evie or Sandi Patty, then I'm not even going to try to sing a solo on the stage because I'm not good enough. I'm not qualified!*

Back when he was a traveling evangelist, Mark and I would actually fight about this. He wanted me to sing before he preached, and I felt he was being cruel and unfair by forcing me to make a fool of myself on the stage. What I didn't realize was that God *had* given me a talent to sing. I *could* perform, but the enemy was trying to prevent me from fulfilling my calling through his lie. He used some powerful emotions to help convince me this lie was true:

Emotions associated with this lie
- *fear*
- *distress*
- *guilt*
- *anxiety*

Does my reaction to my dream remind you of anyone in the Bible? Moses went through the same experience when God called him to lead his people out of Egypt to the Promised Land. After stopping Moses at the burning bush, the Lord told him he had heard the cries of the Israelites and was sending Moses to go before Pharaoh and then lead his people out of Egypt.

> Moses protested to God, "Who am I to appear before Pharaoh? Who am I to lead the people of Israel out of Egypt?"
>
> God answered, "I will be with you. And this is your sign that I am the one who has sent you: When you have brought the people out of Egypt, you will worship God at this very mountain." . . .
>
> But Moses pleaded with the LORD, "O Lord, I'm not very good with words. I never have been, and I'm not now, even though you have spoken to me. I get tongue-tied, and my words get tangled."
>
> Then the LORD asked Moses, "Who makes a person's mouth? Who decides whether people speak or

do not speak, hear or do not hear, see or do not see? Is it not I, the LORD? Now go! I will be with you as you speak, and I will instruct you in what to say."

But Moses again pleaded, "Lord, please! Send anyone else." (Exodus 3:11-12; 4:10-13)

Even biblical heroes like Moses were tempted to believe this Perfect Lie. What would have happened if Moses had refused to obey God? How might the lives of the millions of Hebrews enslaved in Egypt have been affected? Remember, when you refuse to obey God because you assume you're incapable, it is not only your life that is affected by this lie, but also the lives of those who are counting on you for encouragement and leadership.

LIE DETECTOR TEST

Ask yourself the following questions to determine if you believe the Perfect Lie: *I must pull back because I am less capable than others.*

- Do you ever compare yourself to people who seem more talented or successful than you?
- Have you, like Moses, ever balked at something the Lord has asked you to do, deeming yourself inadequate for the task?

Kirbyjon Caldwell, pastor of the largest United Methodist congregation in the United States, has said, "There are two great moments in a person's life: the first is when you were born; the second is when you discover *why* you were born."[8] God has a purpose for your life! And he has graced you with all the talents and abilities you need to fulfill that purpose and calling.

If anyone had an excuse for listening to this Perfect Lie, it would have to be Nick Vujicic, a young Australian who was born without arms and legs. Nick's parents, Christian missionaries who planted a church in Australia eleven months before Nick was born, struggled at first to understand how God could use their son's loss for good. But he has.

Reading in Sunday school about being made in the image of God seemed like a cruel joke to Nick. He seesawed between despair and begging God to grow out his arms and legs for him. He contemplated suicide the year he turned eight. When he was fifteen, though, he ran across a story in the Bible that answered one of his toughest questions.

"When I read the story of the blind man," Nick said, "I began to understand. Jesus said he was born so that the work of God could be revealed through him. That gave me peace. I said, 'Lord, here I am. Use me. Mold me. Make me the man you want me to be.'"

Nick learned to write using the two toes on a partial foot that protrudes from his body. He also learned how to throw tennis balls, answer the phone, walk, and even swim. He invented new ways to shave and brush his own teeth. He earned double degrees in accounting and financial planning by age twenty-one. He became an international motivational speaker and founded Life Without Limbs, an organization for the physically disabled. Nick's mind-set leaves no room for the Perfect Lie "I am unable":

> Despite my physical limitations, I'm living as though I have no limits. . . . I found happiness when I realized that as imperfect as I may be, I am the perfect Nick Vujicic. I am God's creation, designed according to His plan for me. That's not to say there isn't room for improvement. I'm always trying to be better so I can better serve Him and the world![9]

ANTIDOTE TO THE FOURTH PERFECT LIE

Changing old thought patterns is not easy, but it's simple. Let's take a commonly known Scripture and see how we might make it "come alive" to change our neuropathways. Second Corinthians 12:9-10, in fact, is my favorite Bible verse because it describes my life:

> [The Lord] said, "My grace is all you need. My power works best in weakness." So now I am glad to boast about my weaknesses, so that the power of Christ can work through me. That's why I take plea-sure in my weaknesses, and in the insults, hardships,

persecutions, and troubles that I suffer for Christ.
For when I am weak, then I am strong.

It's never been hard for me to see myself as weak. I've always been a small, thin person. I have also been very sweet as well as a scared chicken most of the time. It's easy to see the contrast between my weakness and Christ's strength.

I focus on a particular picture that has helped this Scripture come alive for me. In this image, Jesus Christ is tall, strong, and muscular, which seems appropriate for a carpenter who works with his hands. He is not scared of anything or anyone. He is good-natured as he goes about helping me in my life. Every now and then something may happen, maybe someone is mean to me, which either angers him or makes him sad. In those times, he is more precious to me than ever.

I like to picture Jesus' form as almost invisible and that I am inside of him, fully contained by him because his body is bigger than mine. When I have to lift something, it is really his strength doing the lifting because he's stronger. When I have to walk a long way, it's really his strong legs that are carrying us both to wherever we need to go. No matter what I face, I don't have to be afraid, because my strong guide is actually surrounding me, and I *have his strength*. If people are unfairly upset with me or unjustly critiquing me, they are essentially criticizing Jesus. So I can actually take pleasure in insults, hardships, persecutions, and troubles because they have to go through Jesus to get to me. His power is made perfect in my weakness. When I am weak, then I am strong.

And of course, I am never alone.

I could never have imagined how dramatically my life would be impacted just a few years after I began to overcome this Perfect Lie. For the first several months after my dream, I was tempted to fall back into that lie *I am unable.*

Not me, Lord! I live in the US—in the middle of the US! I know nothing about Africa or human trafficking! Surely, Lord, there is someone else who is more qualified, better able—or at least closer!

But I could not get that dream out of my mind, so I shared it with a few close friends, including my longtime friend Teresa, who owned a clothing boutique a few miles away in Edmond, Oklahoma.

After listening to my dream, she said, "Jennifer, you are not going to believe what I'm about to tell you. Just a few weeks ago, when I was in prayer, God spoke to me about Africa and told me I was going to become involved in a ministry in Africa."

She promised to support me in whatever God had called me to do. Still not believing that God could want *me* to go, I tried unsuccessfully to find someone in Lesotho whom I could help long-distance. When I couldn't make a good connection within Lesotho, I figured, *Well, maybe God just means Africa in general and he gave me the dream to get me to partner with a ministry in Africa.*

I ran this by Danita, another good friend and a missionary to Haiti. She asked me, "Are you telling me that God gave you the specific name of a country in a dream and you are considering spending the rest of your life without ever going to that country? Do you want to wake up every day for the rest of your life and ask: *I wonder what would have happened had I gone to Lesotho?*"

Deeply convicted by her words but still battling fear, I asked her, "Okay, but will you go with me? You are so brave and you moved to Haiti by yourself. You have experience in third-world countries. Will you help me?" She said yes. Another friend, Jana, who ministered with her husband in Botswana, also agreed to visit Lesotho with us.

Eleven and a half months had passed from the time I had the dream to the time I boarded the plane for my first trip to Africa. God providentially opened door after door after door on that trip, and I was even invited to speak in one of the largest churches in Lesotho about my dream and the reason for my visit to their country.

I quickly fell in love with the Basotho people and felt deep compassion for the plight of victimized women and children all around me. Then the real work began: a team joined me in going back to the country several times to complete an extensive feasibility study and develop relationships with government officials, police, and outreach organizations in Lesotho.

In May 2010, the Beautiful Dream Society was officially formed to provide relief and aftercare for victims of human trafficking in Lesotho and South Africa, and to help provide structural prevention and enforce perpetrator accountability. Currently nine of our church members, including two of our former pastors, have followed God's call and moved to Lesotho. The Beautiful Dream Centre, the first shelter for women in Lesotho who have been abused by human trafficking, opened in 2011.

As you can imagine, a few years ago I knew nothing about starting a shelter for victims of human trafficking in Africa; in fact, I had never even had that desire until now. In my own abilities, I am weak. I would never have even considered starting a ministry like this when I was bound and tortured by all the Perfect Lies that I have now exposed. Today when I'm confronted with a challenge that I know my talents and resources can't match, rather than running away, I consider whether this is an instance when God's power is about to be especially magnified.

In fact, I could tell endless stories of how God has demonstrated his strength in the midst of my weakness—times when God has protected us and the ministry despite attempts to harm or deceive us. God has proven himself faithful in every situation!

In the midst of stress and tragedy, we are watching God change the lives of every single surviving victim we have been privileged to serve. Not only does the Beautiful Dream Centre serve as a shelter and transition home for victims of human trafficking, the organization is impacting the legal system that once didn't even acknowledge this crime. In January 2012, we assisted in a historic trial in which the first human trafficking perpetrator of one of the victims in our shelter was convicted and sentenced to fifteen years in prison under a brand-new anti-trafficking law in Lesotho.

MY PICTURE PRAYER EXPERIENCE

When I was struggling with physical pain and weakness after my breakdown, several doctors told me my conditions could never be healed—that I would have to manage them for the rest of my life. In spite of my fear, I could not imagine living the rest of my life with chronic fatigue and weakness. I wanted so badly to battle the lie that I would be incapable of participating in normal activities for the rest of my life. I needed a truthful picture to focus on when my body was exhausted and in pain.

I used Romans 8:11 to create a new image in my mind.

The Spirit of God, who raised Jesus from the dead, lives in you. And just as God raised Christ Jesus from the dead, he will give life to your mortal bodies by this same Spirit living within you.

I had actually memorized this passage in the King James Version, which uses the phrase "quicken your mortal bodies." So, here is how my meditative prayer went:

Father, I thank you that the same Spirit that raised Christ from the dead lives in me and will quicken my mortal body. Father, I thank you that the light, life, and love of Jesus Christ flows through me into every cell of my body and brings life to every part of me.

As I said the words of this prayer, I felt my impatience and frustration leaving. Here is what I saw in my mind: Jesus was lying dead on the stone-cold table of his tomb. This may sound crazy to you, but I would picture myself, almost like a hologram, lying within Jesus' body—my head in his head, my arms in his arms, and my legs in his legs. Next, when I would see Jesus rising from the tomb with the life-giving power of God, I would see myself rising up within him, our hearts beating together. As he would walk out of the tomb with his shoulders back and in full confidence, I, within him, would walk out of the tomb as well. His strength was my strength! I needed nothing else for my life to be complete.

I would envision his healing light and life flowing through every cell of my body. I would picture all of my organs and visualize his life-giving power going from area to area in my body, and everywhere the light touched, the darkness completely disappeared. Taking this time to meditate on specific truthful pictures from the Word of God was the catalyst that began to reprogram my heart and my mind.

YOUR PICTURE PRAYER EXERCISE

Think of a situation in your life in which you feel unqualified or out of your league. Identify the picture that represents that Perfect Lie (your current reality). Now try to imagine what it would look like if you were able to do what needs to be done. Where would you get the strength? Where would you get the ability?

Continue to try different pictures until you find a picture that represents the truth of the situation, which is that you can do anything through Christ who gives you strength.[10]

STATEMENTS TO PONDER

I thank you, Lord, for your power flowing into my heart and life right now.

I believe that your truth has set me free.

I am able to do the things that you have called me to do.

In my weakness, you will reveal your strength through my life!

SCRIPTURES TO PONDER

[The Lord says,] "My grace is all you need. My power works best in weakness." (2 Corinthians 12:9)

When I am weak, then I am strong. (2 Corinthians 12:10)

CHAPTER 8

PERFECT LIE NUMBER FIVE: I AM A TARGET

I MUST PROTECT MYSELF
BECAUSE OTHERS ARE OUT TO GET ME.

Up you arose, Christ victorious.
Your triumph was complete.
Death that failed to rule over us
Lay shattered at your feet.

A thousand welcomes, O blessed King.
A thousand welcomes, eternal Christ.
A thousand welcomes, Lord of Love that set me free.
I welcome you; live in me.

JENNIFER CROW, "THOUSAND WELCOMES," 2006

MY HUSBAND, MARK, was raised in Berryhill, Oklahoma, on the "wrong side" of the river, where the inhabitants had the unlovely nickname of River Rats. His grandfather had been a sharecropper during the Oklahoma Dust Bowl of the 1930s, and like so many other families during that era, he lost everything while trying to provide for his ten children.

127

Mark's father recalls that he got his first pair of shoes when he was five, and that at about that same age, he owned only one shirt, made of wool, which he had to wear every day during the winter and summer. By the time Mark was born, his father was working two or more jobs to provide adequately for his own family, but by then the threat of poverty and the constant fight for survival had cast its shadow over the entire family.

Perhaps no one in his family was more cautious and suspicious than Mark's aunt Lucille. She viewed nearly every event from a negative perspective. She enjoyed attending funerals and even went to pay her respects to people in the community whom she didn't know well. She and her husband lived in a house on a hill that looked down over a greenbelt common area of the community. One morning as Uncle Wayne was reading the paper, Aunt Lucille seemed restless and disturbed by something. She kept getting up from the table to look through the window at some young boys on their way to school.

After several investigative trips to the window, she finally stated with the certainty of Sherlock Holmes, "I'll bet they're all a part of it!"

Uncle Wayne looked up from his paper and asked, "A part of what?"

To which Aunt Lucille quickly replied, "Whatever's going on!"

Perhaps you can relate to this way of viewing the world. If so, you may believe the Perfect Lie:

I must protect myself because others are out to get me.

It's been said that hurting people hurt people, and no one seems immune from being injured in some way beginning at an early age. The fallen world in which we live can be a harsh place, and damaging events take place every day. As a result, we may believe we are a target and need to remain in hiding or attack mode.

And let's face it, difficulties and challenges can make us stronger. The "American spirit"—the fundamental, underlying drive to work hard and make something of ourselves—is drilled into all US citizens. Our national heroes include everyone from the Founding Fathers to those ordinary business travelers who, despite impossible odds, stood up against the terrorists who had hijacked their plane on 9/11. We value hard work, industry, courage, tenacity, and perseverance. We love stories of the underdog winning the day, saving the pretty girl, or defeating the bad guy.

The self-reliant attitude of "pulling yourself up by your own bootstraps" and being united against a common enemy is a good thing when there really is an enemy. But what if you find yourself, like Aunt Lucille, living in a defensive rut of distrust as if *everyone* were out to get you and feeling that you must constantly maintain control so you are not taken advantage of?

Think how easily we fall into this thinking in our everyday lives. How many times have you driven around the mall, circling and circling, looking for a parking place. And then, like an oasis in the desert of parked cars, you see someone pulling out of a space one aisle over! You race to get there, heart pounding, and put your turn signal on, only to have someone else smoothly approach from the other direction—and take your spot!

How do you feel when that happens? (And let's be honest—we've all experienced this at one time or another.) Do you feel as if the other driver is either out to get you or simply doesn't care about you? What kinds of scenarios do you dream up to get back at that person?

A lost parking place isn't a life-or-death matter, but it underscores the competitive nature of many aspects of our lives. How many of us smile sweetly at each other in church on Sunday morning, but then run each other down in order to be the first in line at the buffet for lunch?

Sometimes this lie takes the form of the thought: *People are out to get me, so I must protect myself.* Do you know anyone who uses sarcasm or insults to keep other people at arm's length? They want to hurt the other person before they themselves are hurt. Or what about the man (or woman) who can't commit to a relationship, but perpetually breaks things off when they get too serious? Often that's a self-protective move. At the core such people may believe: *I am a target.*

Whether you feel physically unsafe (as so many Americans did after 9/11) or emotionally unsafe (as do the sarcasm addicts or perpetual relationship saboteurs), the results are the same. You will never be able to draw near to God or to other people until you stop believing the lie.

Emotions associated with this lie
- *judgmentalism*
- *distrust*

Although Mark never experienced the destitute circumstances his grandfather, father, and aunt did, he spent his early years fighting and scrapping for everything he wanted. This defensive posture permeated every area of his physical, emotional, mental, and social life. He describes the trauma of having to pass the infamous "Fight Corner" every day when walking to and from elementary school, middle school, and high school. His fights and playground scuffles (some of which he won; some of which he didn't) have been the fodder of many humorous sermon illustrations! Although he is tall, muscular, and fit now, he didn't hit his first significant growth spurt until he was sixteen, so he perceived the world as a tough place and himself as an easy target for bullies and others looking for a fight. He was sure everyone was out to get him, and he was ready to defend himself at any moment.

You know, you can live your whole life in a perpetually protective mode. Of course, it's good to have healthy boundaries. But when those boundaries go a little haywire and you begin to protect yourself from the good as well as the bad, that's unhealthy. Ultimately, you may just dry up and die in an emotional desert.

LIE DETECTOR TEST

Ask yourself the following questions to determine whether you believe the fifth Perfect Lie: *I must protect myself because others are out to get me.*

- Do you tend to view life as a competition? Do you find yourself in a constant state of tension, fighting to get the good parking place or to be first in the grocery store checkout line?
- Do you think of other people as basically benevolent— or as out to get you? Are you more likely to smile or scowl at strangers?
- How trusting are you in your relationships? Do you believe the best about your spouse, your children, and your friends? Or are you constantly waiting for the "other shoe to drop"?
- Have you been hurt in the past? How have you been able to deal with that hurt? Even if you have forgiven the person who hurt you, what repercussions, if any, still haunt you in your current relationships?

Jesus often used pictures or parables to illustrate truths about his protection and love for his children. In John 10, Jesus describes a wall or fence of protection around his sheep (who represent us, his children). He tells us we will know when a thief or robber is trying to break in and climb over the wall to harm us. He tells us we will distinguish the one trying to hurt us from the Good Shepherd who is rightfully entering through the gate. Jesus says we will know his voice, which is there to help us, not hurt us, and we will follow him.

My favorite part of this picture is when Jesus says that even if a wolf tries to attack the sheep, the Good Shepherd, who loves them, will sacrifice his life to save and protect them. He reiterates: "I know my own sheep, and they know me. . . . So I sacrifice my life for the sheep" (John 10:14-15).

Remember the tale of Little Red Riding Hood and the Big Bad Wolf? None of us want the wolf to show up in our lives. The Bible identifies a similar enemy, the devil, who comes "to steal and kill and destroy" (John 10:10). Now, picture your own life with a high-tech electrical fence erected all around you, designed to keep the Big Bad Wolf out. Every time the wolf even approaches your fence, he gets the shock of his life!

But despite that fence, the wolf keeps prowling, looking for a weak spot. Even though he can't get in, he circles your life, growling. He starts throwing out lies: "I'm going to get you eventually" or "You can't hide in there forever." And you begin to think, *I really need to beef up this fence. I'm not sure it's strong enough!* And so you start trying to build up your wall, fortifying it more and more—even though you're perfectly safe. The problem is, you have now locked everyone out—maybe Little Red Riding Hood with her basket of goodies and even your Lord, who wants more than anything to give you his peace and joy. But he can't get in.

Can you see the analogy? Yes, the devil is real. Yes, we need to be aware of the need to stay under God's protection to keep evil from infiltrating our lives and stealing all the good things God has for us. But we can rest in the peace of knowing that our Good Shepherd is the one who has given us the ultimate protection and victory. Jesus even goes so far as to say that he is the gate into the enclosure of protection. He states that those who come in through him will be protected and that they will go in and out of the gate freely and will find good pastures (John 10:9).

But if the boundaries we erect are based on fear rather than on trust in the protection that God offers us, we can end up losing out on the blessings he wants to shower on our lives—including an amazing relationship with him.

Listen to what the Bible says our posture should be toward others, even those who may mean us harm:

> Dear friends, never take revenge. Leave that to the righteous anger of God. For the Scriptures say, "I will take revenge; I will pay them back," says the LORD. Instead, "If your enemies are hungry, feed them. If they are thirsty, give them something to drink. In doing this, you will heap burning coals of shame on their heads." Don't let evil conquer you, but conquer evil by doing good. (Romans 12:19-21)

What matters is not keeping everybody out because "everybody's out to get me" and "I've got to protect number one." What matters is giving of yourself and doing good. What matters is trusting that God is protecting you and that he is not going to put more on you than you can handle with him by your side. Evil cannot conquer you. Other people might shoot arrows of hostility, jealousy, or anger at you, but remember: vengeance is God's, and he will repay—on your behalf. You don't have to protect yourself—he will.

At one point years ago, I noticed that I was being hurt by things that really shouldn't have hurt me. I felt constantly assaulted and lived my life with adrenaline pumping through my body, ready to defend myself and counterattack! Even when I knew the other person hadn't meant to hurt me and that God loved me enough to make up for what others in my life couldn't give me, I struggled to let go of my hurt feelings.

I had to come up with a way to relinquish my pain and relax when I felt attacked. I knew that I needed to replace the picture that was in my mind—that of a wounded, crying, defensive Jennifer—with a new and better picture that was based on the truth of God's Word.

One day I thought of a silly children's cartoon that helped me with this. Remember Casper the Friendly Ghost? He could walk through walls and move his arms through objects; in other words, nothing could touch him. I began to picture myself just like that. When hurts came at me like arrows, they would come into my body, but they couldn't touch the "real" me. They would pass right on through me and land safely on the other side. I acknowledged the hurt in the moment—I didn't try to deny it—but then I let it go without fighting back at the person who had hurt me.

It is not that I don't care what people say or do to me. But

I allow the *hurt* that their words or actions cause to pass right on through me. I have learned to let it go. As a result, I don't have to be on the defensive anymore!

ANTIDOTE TO THE FIFTH PERFECT LIE

One of the best-known sayings of Jesus comes from Luke 23:34, which Jesus spoke as he was dying on the cross:

> Jesus said, "Father, forgive them, for they don't know what they are doing."

It would be difficult to find anyone who had more reason to feel targeted and attacked than Jesus Christ when he was beaten, whipped, mocked, and crucified. He had spent his days showing God's love to everyone he met, whether healing the sick and oppressed or teaching about his Father's mercy. Imagine living such a perfect life that you never have to apologize even for unintentional slips of the tongue: "Oops! Sorry, I didn't mean to say that!" or "I didn't mean it that way." Yet Jesus was executed for exhibiting the very loving behavior that challenged the corrupt world system he came to illuminate. Jesus, of all people, could have been justifiably vulnerable to the Perfect Lie: *I must protect myself because others are out to get me.*

There is nothing more discouraging and unfair than being unjustly attacked. That's why I can relate to the humorous description my husband gave in one of his sermons of what he would like to have done had *he* been Christ on the cross—perfect in every way, without sin, and yet publicly attacked and humiliated. Mark emphatically described how he would have been tempted to dispatch some choice lightning bolts aimed at just the right people to show them who was boss of the universe! I think we can all relate to this feeling. It is natural for us as humans to want to fight back. And yet Christ showed us a better way.

When reading about the Crucifixion, I have sometimes skimmed over Luke 23:34, missing the power of these words in this familiar story. I certainly have been in awe of his response: *Wasn't he amazing for being so forgiving? Wow! How could he do that?* But when I meditated further, I realized Jesus could give me the power to apply his antidote to my sinful tendency to remain stuck in the mode of judgment, defense, and attack.

How *could* Jesus ask God to pardon his assailants? What did *he know* that gave him the power to forgive? I suspect that in those final moments suspended on the cross, his flesh searing with pain, he must have observed and examined the inner landscape of the soul of each soldier, priest, official, and member of the crowd. He must have seen every individual story from that person's unique perspective. Since he was the all-knowing God, he knew their histories. He understood their upbringings. He identified their beliefs. He evaluated their thinking. He experienced their pain. He discerned the exact hurts they were feeling at that moment. He recognized they were only doing what they thought was right and effective at the time. He viewed the scenario from their perspective and realized most of the people didn't know they were killing the Son of God. He comprehended all of this, and he experienced compassion toward them. That same compassion gave him the power to willingly die in their place—and in my place and your place.

Even though we are not omnipotent or all knowing, our Creator has given us the ability to empathize with and "put ourselves in the shoes" of another person. We have the ability to interpret the signals others give to help us determine their thought processes, actions, and behaviors. In other words, we can mentalize, which is simply the ability, when interacting with someone else, to see the situation from our own perspective while also working to comprehend the situation from the other person's viewpoint. Scientists and psychologists have learned that most people begin to learn empathy from infancy—at least those with a primary caregiver who mentalized or determined what was going on in their little minds and what their bodies were crying out for throughout the day and night. Psychologists have learned that in general, the more a primary caregiver empathizes with an infant, the more that baby learns to mentalize or empathize with others. With skill and practice, we can continue to fine-tune the art of empathy and mentalization, which can lead to compassion, love, and peace toward other people, including those who may hurt us.

So when I am facing a situation where I feel that I am a target and my instincts want to protect, defend, and attack—assuming it's not an emergency, of course—I take some time for meditative prayer. I think of the story of Jesus dying on the cross. I know that unlike him, I am not perfect. I have sinned. I may not be guilty of the things that I'm being targeted for at the moment, but without the forgiveness of Christ and the atonement of his blood, I deserve to be on that cross. I have been unkind. I have been selfish. I have lied. I have cheated. I have stolen.

I look around at those whose insults or slights have wounded me. And then I ask, *What is the truth of this picture?* I endeavor to see the offenders as they might have been when they were nine or ten years old, fresh faced and excited about their lives ahead. I imagine them to be like my son or daughter. I ask myself: *What are they feeling right now?*

I take into consideration the facts that I know about the circumstances, along with what I sense by the power of the Holy Spirit and what my imagination intuitively tells me to investigate, and I contemplate the source of their own pain. I still feel my pain, but I try to experience their pain at the same time. I imagine how they may have sought to find relief by lashing out at me. I see they are only doing what I'm tempted to do, which is to protect myself from further pain. As I begin to sense their hurt, even though I am in pain myself because of them, the Lord gives me the power to forgive out of the deep compassion I feel for their hurt. This compassion does not take away my pain, because love can hurt. However, compassion diffuses the pain. This new way of looking at the situation helps me to let the pain go and allow it to dissipate, so that it is no longer destructive but instead is strengthening to my soul.

MY PICTURE PRAYER EXPERIENCE

When I began learning to change the pictures of my heart to reflect the truth, I tended to focus on memories from the distant past. Eventually, though, I began trying this form of meditative prayer on recent events. After all, I store new information each day in the form of pictures, so it is important that I deal with these events too.

I find some people in my life difficult to deal with—as I'm sure you do. They can be demanding and volatile. I'm always tempted to do everything possible to avoid making them angry and keep them calm.

I finally realized that trying to please such people as a defensive coping mechanism is fighting a losing battle. While I could control my speech and outward behavior to keep the peace, their words, tone of voice, or actions often left me feeling hurt. What could I do to end the second-guessing that plagued and tormented me after an encounter with one of these toxic people? Let me show you what diffusing the Perfect Lie and finding the truth looked like for me.

I'm going to call such a person "the Chihuahua." She constantly nags and finds fault. No matter what I do, it never seems to be good enough. I could do ten things right, but she will mention only the one thing I did wrong. The Chihuahua is not content to let me do things my own way or to have my own opinion. She feels compelled to correct me for my own good. She may or may not intend to manipulate, and her criticism may even contain some truth, but her objective seems to be pointing out every sin of omission or commission.

After an encounter with the Chihuahua, I asked myself during my prayer time, *What are you feeling right now? What lie are you believing?* I realized that I was feeling attacked and defensive. I thought, *She is out to get me and will completely gobble up all that I really am if I do not defend myself!* I even asked God, *How can this be a lie when it feels so true?*

I thought about how I felt when I was around her. It felt to me as if she were huge and in my face, screaming all of my faults and failures at me. She seemed so big and so loud and so intimidating that I wanted to put my hands up to my face to protect myself.

I prayed and asked God to show me a truthful picture of what was really happening. How could I find peace in this situation? Where was Jesus during these encounters?

Here is the mental picture that helped me let this go: I picture Jesus and me having an intimate, loving conversation with one another. He is seated and I am at his feet with my chin resting in his lap, looking up at him. He strokes my hair as we talk about nothing . . . and everything. We speak like old friends, sometimes laughing, sometimes quiet, but completely at peace. Then in walks my nemesis, and immediately she starts shouting at me. She is so loud that I want to take the remote control and turn down the volume. So in my imagination (in which I can do whatever I want) I am able to turn down the sound. Not only does her voice get softer, she also begins getting smaller and smaller, as if she's a character out of *Alice in Wonderland*. (I do have a vivid imagination!) There . . . that's better—but I still hear an annoying, unrelenting whining noise. I turn down the volume even more until finally this person is microscopic. And although she shouts at the top of her lungs, her words are about as noticeable as the yips of a miniature Chihuahua, whose soft "peeps" reach my ears only every now and then.

This picture actually makes me laugh out loud during my prayer time. It fills me with joy. This is not an intimidating picture, but a funny, peaceful one. This is an image of the truth—Jesus and me enjoying each other's presence while a microscopic person is ranting and raving about who knows what. The truth is that my relationship with him is much bigger and more influential in my life than any comments she may have, and her opinion about me pales in comparison to what Jesus thinks about me.

Okay, let's get back to real life for a minute. "All well and good," you may say, "but what about when I am *in* that situation? Are you telling me just to space out and go to my 'happy place'?"

What I am saying is that you need to become cognizant of the truth of the bigger picture. Approaching this situation with the proper frame of reference is essential. You must get in touch with the true perspective of what you are dealing with so that you are not pulled into an unhealthy thought pattern. If you suspect you are dealing with a truly manipulative person, I recommend you read *Who's Pulling Your Strings?* by Harriet Braiker. This book gives some wonderful, simple steps to counter the effects of a manipulative person. I have read this book several times and employed these tools on numerous occasions, but if you often feel like a target, I can tell you that many of the battles must be fought between your ears and in the pictures of your heart and mind.

YOUR PICTURE PRAYER EXERCISE

How does it make you feel when you have dealings with someone who seems "out to get you"? When was the first time you can remember feeling that way? Identify what that picture looks like and use the truth to diffuse the power of that image. Is this individual really trying to hurt you? Can this individual really hurt you? Try to see the situation from their perspective in order to see if you can find any compassion for them. Try visualizing yourself safely in God's care, and then take the remote and "turn down their volume." When you find an image that gives you comfort and peace, dwell on that image for five minutes.

STATEMENTS TO PONDER

I am safe in God's love and free to love other people.

I can allow myself to enjoy life.

I can choose not to let my past hurts control me today or in the future.

I cannot control the world around me, but I choose to respond with kindness and gentleness.

God is always there to defend me, and he fills my heart with peace.

God has set me apart to bless me, his child, with his abundance and protection.

SCRIPTURES TO PONDER

Do not let yourself be overcome by evil, but overcome (master) evil with good. (Romans 12:21, AMP)

This I declare about the LORD:
He alone is my refuge, my place of safety;
  he is my God, and I trust him. (Psalm 91:2)

He shall give His angels charge over you,
To keep you in all your ways.
In their hands they shall bear you up,
Lest you dash your foot against a stone.
  (Psalm 91:11-12, NKJV)

CHAPTER 9

PERFECT LIE NUMBER SIX: I AM NOT ANGRY

I MUST AVOID CONFLICT
BECAUSE EXPRESSING MY ANGER IS WRONG.

All for your glory, we'll sing your song,
Blaze like stars, we're pressing on.
We'll finish strong.
All for your glory to win the prize,
Holding fast your Word of life.
We'll finish strong.

JENNIFER CROW, CHRIS CROW, AND JARON NIX,
"FINISH STRONG," 2007

WHEN OUR FOURTH CHILD, Joseph, was eight months old, I was offered the job of worship leader at our church, where Mark served as youth pastor. My immediate response was that it was out of the question. After all, I was still nursing a baby and had three other children under the age of five. After I declined the job offer, though, the Lord began to speak to my heart, and I felt as if I heard him say, *Jennifer, if you could do this, would you want to?*

Frankly, the idea of leading the band, scheduling volunteers, choosing the music, and leading singing at four services a week sounded very appealing. Of course I wanted to lead worship. I loved music; I loved God; and although I had helped Mark by leading worship for his youth groups, this would be my first opportunity as the key leader in worship for adults. I opened my mind and began to think what life would be like if we could work this out.

The pastor and I began to negotiate and were able to agree on a salary and schedule that would allow me to hire a weekly housekeeper, do all the administrative work from home, and line up someone to come to our home on Sunday mornings to get the children ready for church while I was at early rehearsal.

In the midst of our deliberations, I met with the pastor for a formal interview. He asked one question that had me momentarily stumped: "How do you handle conflict?"

Man, that's a hard one. My mind's wheels were turning, searching for incidences of interpersonal strife so I could answer his question. When I think back on the answer I gave him, I want to laugh out loud at how it must have sounded, but I was dead serious: "I can't recall any conflicts. I get along with everyone."

I'm not sure what our pastor thought, but he gave me the job anyway!

What I didn't realize then was that I had been blinded by the Perfect Lie:

I must avoid conflict
because expressing my anger is wrong.

When most people think of anger, they equate it with someone like Almira Gulch, the character who shows up at Uncle Henry and Aunt Em's farm in one of the opening scenes of *The Wizard of Oz.*

After furiously pedaling her bicycle to the front gate, Miss Gulch commands, "Mr. Gale! I want to see you and your wife right away about Dorothy."

Miss Gulch explains that Dorothy's dog, Toto, bit her. "I'm all but lame from the bite on my leg," she complains. "That dog's a menace to the community. I'm taking him to the sheriff and make sure he's destroyed."

Dorothy protests, "Auntie Em, Uncle Henry, you won't let her, will you?"

Uncle Henry responds, "Of course we won't, will we, Em?" while looking questioningly at his wife.

Aunt Em suggests, "How would it be if she keeps him tied up? He's really gentle—with gentle people, that is."

Miss Gulch's anger isn't satisfied: "If you don't hand over that dog, I'll bring a damage suit that'll take your whole farm. There's a law protecting folks against dogs that bite."

Aunt Em remains seated during this violent exchange. Seemingly calm and serenely uninvolved, she instructs, "We can't go against the law, Dorothy. I'm afraid poor Toto will have to go."

Dorothy gives full vent to her anger and begins to wail,

"I won't let you take him! You go away, you . . . ! Oooh, I'll bite you myself! . . . You wicked old witch!"

Miss Gulch jerks out the basket she brought to place Toto in and tries to snatch the dog out of Dorothy's arms while Aunt Em and Uncle Henry look on. As Dorothy desperately glances from one guardian to the other, she realizes there is no one to defend her and dashes tearfully from the scene.

While the witchy Miss Gulch has no trouble expressing her rage, Aunt Em struggles to deny the anger building inside of her. It seems that perhaps she's reached her boiling point when she emphatically declares, "Almira Gulch, just because you own half the county doesn't mean you have the power to run the rest of us!" At long last, Aunt Em seems ready to stand up to the town bully.

"For twenty-three years I've been dying to tell you what I thought of you," Aunt Em exclaims, "and now—well, being a Christian woman, I can't say it!"

Notice that Aunt Em feels anger; the difference between her and Miss Gulch is that Aunt Em stuffs her anger as a way to avoid conflict while Miss Gulch seems to revel in her ability to intimidate others.

If you struggle with this lie as well, you may recognize some of the emotions beneath it.

Emotions associated with this lie

- *complacency*
- *fear of conflict*
- *indifference*

Aunt Em comes across as a "holier than thou" individual who is above getting angry and who would give up a little dog to an abusive woman just because she believes it is wrong to show righteous anger. Imagine if she had calmly but consistently communicated her anger every time Miss Gulch had tried to manipulate the situation for her own benefit. Isn't it likely that the situation with Toto would never have progressed to where it did because Miss Gulch would not have been as confident in her ability to intimidate?

LIE DETECTOR TEST

Ask yourself the following questions to determine whether you have believed the Perfect Lie: *I must avoid conflict because expressing my anger is wrong.*

- Do you always strive to keep the peace, no matter what?
- Are there difficult people in your life whom you try to please to avoid conflict with them?
- Do you have a feeling that it is wrong for you to ever be angry?

I was extremely vulnerable to believing this lie for much of my life. As a coping mechanism, I tried to keep my life and my feelings in perfect equilibrium at all times. If I didn't acknowledge conflict, I thought, then perhaps it would just go away. I became very good at keeping the peace. On the surface, this may have seemed like a positive trait, but I discovered that people resented my unwillingness to acknowledge their anger if they were displeased with me or a decision I had made. They took my unwillingness to engage in conflict as a sign that I didn't really care about their feelings.

As a young person, when I read the passages where Jesus confronted the scribes and Pharisees and physically knocked over the merchants' tables in the Temple, I thought, *Wow, that wasn't very Christian!* That's because I believed the lie that real Christians never get angry.

This lie is unique among the nine Perfect Lies. While the other eight falsehoods lead people to feel worse about themselves, when people tell themselves this lie, they are often viewing themselves or their circumstances as "better" than they really are. That's one reason why discerning this lie can be so difficult. Not only that, but like the other deceptions, this one can be tough to identify because it may have some basis in truth.

On the surface, maintaining peace at all costs can seem like a positive characteristic. After all, the Bible says, "Do all that you can to live in peace with everyone" (Romans 12:18). Doesn't that mean anger, which nearly always disrupts peace, is a sin? Isn't it better to turn the other cheek?

Those who fall victim to this lie tend to believe that Christianity equals "nice." Yet if you read your Bible closely, you'll see that "niceness" isn't included in Galatians 5's list of the fruit of the Spirit ("kind," yes; "nice," no). If you doubt that God is comfortable confronting sin, just consider this passage from Revelation:

I know your deeds, that you are neither cold nor
hot. I wish you were either one or the other! So,
because you are lukewarm—neither hot nor cold—
I am about to spit you out of my mouth. You say, "I
am rich; I have acquired wealth and do not need a
thing." But you do not realize that you are wretched,
pitiful, poor, blind and naked. (3:15-17, NIV)

God is speaking directly to a group of people who are
in denial about their situation. Many of them were likely
decent, "nice" people—yet it appears their comfort prevented
them from expressing much passion about anything, including
God himself.

When we seek to keep the peace by going along, we may
be guilty of passive compromise, which displeases God. We
prevent serious problems from being acknowledged and
addressed, and we alienate those who see the problem and
refuse to live in denial. Just consider the parent who, by
rationalizing and denying his or her own feelings, enables
the abuse perpetrated by the other parent. Obviously, to the
child, this is a big deal! The abuse is something to get angry
about, not ignore!

Righteous anger is what drove abolitionists to speak up in
the eighteenth century, and I believe it's what gives momentum to the pro-life movement today. My husband and I first
became involved in the pro-life movement back in the late
1980s because we were moved by the righteous anger of some
Christians who actively opposed abortion. In 1988, I read a

brief news story about Christian protestors who were peace-fully blocking the doors to the abortion clinics in Atlanta during the Democratic National Convention, which was being held in that city. One of the protestors explained they were driven to act because man's law was in direct violation of God's law, which seeks to protect all life. Because of their anger over the unjust killing of unborn infants, these men and women were willing to take a stand.

I hadn't really thought much about the abortion issue before, but their anger fueled a similar reaction in me. I couldn't look at my own toddler and infant without hurting for the babies who were being aborted. After doing some research, I discovered an abortion clinic right in Tulsa, not far from my own home in the middle of conservative America. When I learned about an upcoming National Day of Rescue, I began praying that the Lord would get someone involved—perhaps even Mark. Although I told him about my idea that someone in Tulsa should organize the Christians to stage a "rescue" (a peaceful demonstration of civil disobedience where individuals sit and block the doors of the abortion clinic), weeks went by without an answer from him.

As the date for the national protest drew near, I debated about what I should do. I wanted to help save human lives and bring to light the horrors of abortion. I believed that tres-passing on private property to prevent the taking of human life would be as justifiable as breaking down a neighbor's door if you saw flames and smoke pouring from their win-dows. Yet I knew that not everyone agreed with me and that if I sat in front of the abortion clinic to prevent children from being killed that day, I would probably be arrested. What would all the people at my church think? Would my husband ever be able to get another job as a minister? What would happen to my children if I went to jail?

Not long before the National Day of Rescue, I told Mark that I had made my decision. I would be on the steps of that abortion clinic whether anyone joined me or not. My poor husband sighed and looked a bit frustrated. After a long pause, he responded in true gentlemanly fashion, "Well . . . if you are going to get arrested, I'm not going to let you do it by yourself. And we might as well get some others to join us."

And that was the beginning of Operation Rescue Tulsa. My mom and dad drove up from Texas to stay with our children. Mark and I, along with about sixty friends, went to the clinic before dawn, sitting in front of the front and back doors so that people who wanted to get into the clinic would have to walk through a crowd of people sitting six or seven deep. We did not intend to touch, harm, or prevent anyone from entering; we were there simply to offer adoption, financial, and medical care resources to women. There were many positive outcomes, which resulted from our seemingly radical response to our anger. No abortions were performed that day, many more people became aware and involved in the heartbreakingly overlooked issue, and one couple who participated in the rescue became so passionate about the tragedy that they began to picket regularly at this abortion clinic and eventually adopted a baby who had been scheduled to be aborted!

Oh yes . . . and we were all given citations for trespassing and ordered to appear in court at a later date. Our actions were reported on the news by the local broadcast affiliates, as well as on the front page of the *Tulsa World*. In the midst of all the publicity, many of our friends and coworkers seemed unsure how to react and avoided us for a while.

As our court date approached, I did some research on prenatal development that I thought might convince the judge that our actions were justified. I had the opportunity to testify before the judge, and though I was anxious, I felt I'd presented a reasonable, persuasive case for trespassing.

Then as I nervously stood before him, he impassively delivered his verdict, "Jennifer Crow—guilty!"

I was flabbergasted. The state of Oklahoma thought I was wrong! I had innocently supposed the court and my fellow Americans would arise in our support when they heard the testimony of their peers about the truth of the development of babies in the womb. I had naively hoped our trespassing case would plant a seed to overturn Roe v. Wade. I was devastated when that didn't happen.

In that instance, my righteous anger didn't lead to the outcome I wanted. Yet I don't regret speaking out. In fact, sometimes I think, as intimidating as it was to stand up to the laws of our country, it can be even more difficult to stand up to one person. Let's face it: conflict is uncomfortable, and we can be fearful that our anger might bring our relationships or us to a difficult spot. But our attempts to avoid disagreement at all costs can cross into passivity and complacency.

That gives us only two choices whenever problems emerge: compromise or denial. We adopt a defensive response as a way to protect ourselves from pain, hurt, and suffering, and to avoid conflict, disagreements, or disapproval from others. Those who believe this lie are extremely vulnerable to manipulation. Even if they vehemently disagree with someone on an issue or are troubled by another's behavior, they will keep their displeasure to themselves to avoid conflict. It's easier just to go along.

I learned firsthand how tempting this can be while working as worship leader at the church where I'd told the pastor I never got into conflicts with other people. My statement was proven wrong during an uncomfortable incident with the church's audio technician—I'll call her Alice.

Alice was businesslike and seemed to perform her duties responsibly. Yet she made it clear to me that running the sound board was her territory, that she had been doing it for years *her way* (which was, of course, the *right* way), and that she didn't take kindly to anyone trying to change her methods.

One of my goals each week was to create the most effective, beautiful worship experience for each person in the congregation so they could connect with God during worship. I didn't want them to be distracted by players playing wrong notes, vocalists singing off pitch, or audio sound that was full of feedback or annoying frequencies. I'm not sure what

Alice's objective was, but it didn't take long for it to become painfully obvious that Alice and I were not on the same track.

One Sunday morning, we had a bit of a rough rehearsal before church, so I was onstage during the sound check giving direction to Alice, who was back in the sound booth. The auditorium was buzzing with volunteers who were getting into position for serving, and people were beginning to find their seats. As I was trying to work with Alice to resolve the problems I heard in my monitors, Alice blurted out, "Would you just shut up and sing!"

Wow. There was dead silence in the auditorium. I think the volunteers and early arrivers were as shocked as I was! I could feel the anger and hurt rising as my face flushed. I wanted to burst into tears and sprint off the stage, but I instinctively recognized that wouldn't be the most effective response. My Polly Peacemaker self was momentarily paralyzed by the attack.

After a deafening pause that seemed to last forever, my husband, who was one of the singers onstage, broke the awkward silence by speaking up and trying to resolve the situation. My mind was reeling. I don't remember how we got through the remainder of that rehearsal and worship service, but my thoughts were definitely not following the sermon that morning.

I hated that having to resolve conflict was part of my job. I would have preferred just to fall back into my familiar lie "I am not angry" and go on as if everything was fine. Even though I didn't recognize the lie at the time, I knew that if I backed down and didn't confront Alice, I would lose all self-respect, her respect, and my ability to be an effective leader. I requested a meeting with Alice and the pastor to try to resolve the situation. Unfortunately, the result was not what I had hoped for, but I have to give myself credit for being extremely brave, facing my fear, and trying my best to kindly confront someone.

I have since learned that when a person is in a position of leadership, he or she can never make everyone happy. Our family of seven can rarely agree on where we want to go to eat; how much less could hundreds or thousands of people agree with everything a pastor or worship leader does or says!

Believing that we must avoid conflict because expressing our anger is wrong can lead to terrible outcomes. This lie ultimately fails the very people who try to live by it. As much as we may deny anger, it always eventually surfaces. Many times, this suppressed anger can even manifest itself as disease in the body caused by stress.

ANTIDOTE TO THE SIXTH PERFECT LIE

One of the first Scriptures I memorized was "Do not let the sun go down on your anger" (Ephesians 4:26, NASB). This simple Scripture, I've found, promotes excellent mental health. As a new Christian in my early teens, I would lay my head down at night and think, *Who am I angry with?* If someone came to mind, I would purposefully choose to forgive that person to the best of my ability and then would drift peacefully off to sleep. Of course, the problems and issues we have as teens often seem to pale in comparison with the challenges that emerge throughout adulthood.

At some point I began to suppress my response to anger. I thought anger was bad or wrong because I didn't understand from this simple verse that it was okay to be angry as long as anger did not control me. Let's look at the verse in context:

> And "don't sin by letting anger control you." Don't let the sun go down while you are still angry, for anger gives a foothold to the devil. (Ephesians 4:26-27)

Notice the verse says, "Don't sin by letting anger *control* you" (emphasis mine). The feeling of anger is *not* a sin; it is an emotional response that can happen to anyone. Remember that all emotions are variables of six basic human emotions, one of which is anger. This feeling helps us respond quickly and appropriately to our environment. In itself, it is neither positive nor negative.

If your neighbor loudly berates your teenage son for stepping on her pristine lawn, it's normal to feel a flash of anger. In this case, anger can motivate you to find out the facts and, if necessary, stand up in your son's defense. Anger is not helpful, however, if you stuff it or if you seethe about your neighbor's harsh words for days.

To help Christians understand the difference between appropriate and destructive anger, the apostle Paul compared it to the rising and setting of the sun. Just as the sun rises and then sets in a cycle every day, at times you will feel justifiable anger rising within you. You *want* to feel anger if someone is attacking an innocent person unjustly. On the other hand, you must let the anger go by the end of the day (or at the appropriate time) because long-lasting, unresolved anger will hurt only you, the one harboring the anger.

"Letting go of anger" does *not* mean you no longer respond to the situation that initially caused the anger. You can still respond effectively to the situation over the following days without the *feeling* of anger. You may even get angry again (like the rising of the sun), but then you need to let go of the anger again to remain effective, letting your emotions rise and fall as God intended.

Paul warns in verse 27 that "anger gives a foothold to the devil." The implication here is that *long-lasting anger* (extending more than a day) definitely opens the door to harm and evil.

So how do you acknowledge your anger (a neutral emotion—neither good nor bad) and then channel it appropriately before letting it dissipate? By thoughtfully meditating and then developing a truthful picture based on the simple Scripture "Don't let the sun go down on your anger," you can learn to respond effectively to feelings of anger. Let me illustrate what this looks like for me.

As I sit quietly with my hands on my heart or in a position of prayer, I ask myself, *What am I feeling?* (Or *What was I feeling a few hours ago?*) If I acknowledge that I am feeling angry, I see my anger as hot and flaming like the sun. I see the green hills and fields flourishing under the life-giving power of the sun as I look out across the landscape of my soul from my hill of meditation. I feel the anger. I acknowledge the anger. I purposefully and consciously make my rational mind explore the reasons for the anger in a nonjudgmental way. I don't chastise myself for feeling the anger, but I also don't instantly let the anger turn to hatred toward someone else.

As I explore my reasons for the anger, I know that the daylight hours are the time to work in the green fields and hills of my soul. I ask myself, *What actions do I need to take during these daylight hours to respond effectively to this anger?* Do I need to have a conversation with someone? Do I need to get some advice? Do I need to send an e-mail? Do I need to call the police or get help? Do I need to make a list of possible options to respond effectively to this anger? Even if I can't bring actual resolution to the situation itself, I try to bring some form of closure to my feelings of anger by determining what action I can take. If I am unsure what the appropriate action items will be, then my action item becomes making time to think through the action items again tomorrow. I don't ignore the anger. I don't try to escape having to deal with the situation that caused the anger. It is daylight, and it is time for me to work effectively.

But then, as always happens, the sun gets lower in the sky and it is time for me to prepare to rest. I cannot rest while I am feeling angry. Since I have investigated my anger during the daylight hours and have determined a plan of action, I am confident I no longer *need* my anger to motivate me to respond. I have already decided what I will do, and *I will do it*, so I can let the anger go as the shadows fall. I can enjoy my evening with my family. I can enjoy my rest. I can let go of the angry emotion, knowing I'll take the important follow-up action the next day.

MY PICTURE PRAYER EXPERIENCE

I start my five- to ten-minute meditation session with this question: *What am I feeling right now?* If the answer is anger, I ask: *Is this righteous, justifiable anger, as Jesus had; or is this sinful, selfish anger?*

Then I consider, *What is the truth about this picture?* Sometimes I determine that there has been a legitimate misunderstanding between another person and me. At other times I recognize that a person has responded out of hurt or immaturity and might be open to dialogue. Sometimes, however, it seems the person is not interested in a win-win resolution.

If someone has attacked or lashed out at me verbally, I try to find a picture to help me get relief. I know I need to forgive that person just as Jesus forgave those who jeered at him as he was dying on the cross. He cried out, "Father, forgive them, for they don't know what they are doing" (Luke 23:34). So, like Jesus, I pray and see myself asking God to please forgive the person, because he or she is unaware of the sin being committed. Even if the person has maliciously hurt me, I still decide to forgive them. After all, I am not the judge—only God can judge.

Forgiving, however, does not mean that I have to put my trust in or spend time with that person. Just as God knows he will spend eternity separated from some people whom he created and loves dearly, there will be people in my life who, because of their choice or this sinful, evil world we live in, are not going in the same direction as I am.

When I told one of my friends about this type of meditative prayer, she used it to find healing from the hurt and anger she had stuffed after her parents' divorce when she was twelve. After her dad was unfaithful to her mom, my friend felt horrible for her mom and conflicted over the situation. As the older child, she also felt compelled to try and keep the peace for the sake of her mom and little brother. She traces much of her inner turmoil back to a family dinner at the home of her new stepmother's parents:

> As we sat at the table with my father, his new wife, Carol, and her parents, we were two children, ages twelve and six, feeling very awkward and fearful because our lives had just been ripped apart by divorce. There we were, at the table, with laughter, forced smiles, and conversation on the outside, but on the inside, at least from our point of view, it was a miserable experience. We were supposed to act as if we were one big, happy family and yet we were

sitting with strangers whom we barely knew and were being expected to enter into the conversation.

As this loud Italian family was talking all around us, my father, in order to cover for our lack of conversation, said, "You'll have to excuse my children; they're just not used to all this noise." This was a completely false statement—we were perfectly well-adjusted kids—our world had just been rocked due to my father's betrayal. Why was he blaming the discomfort of the situation on us? I initially felt anger, but as my father spoke, I began to see myself through his eyes as an awkward individual, unable to handle myself socially—a tongue-tied outsider who was not a part of the "happy" crowd. That humiliating picture became emblazoned in my mind and stuck with me as a defining moment in my life.

From that point on, my friend felt intimidated and uneasy whenever she had to speak in the presence of men. The practice of meditative prayer drew her back to this memory, the first time she ever remembered feeling this way.

Many years later, as I was trying to find the truth of this picture during my prayer time, I asked, "Where were you, Lord, during this situation? And if you had been there in the flesh, what would you have been doing?"

As I imagined my heavenly Father's response and where he would be and what he would do, I saw Jesus there with us. He was not observing from afar, but he was engaged with us, at the dinner table right in the midst of our pain. He was sitting between my brother and me with his arms around us, but his arms were like the wings of a giant eagle. When my dad made the comment about us not being used to the noise, I saw Jesus rise from the table and say these words: "Ah, no . . . these two are used to plenty of noise!" And then, as he rose and lifted his giant arms, everyone at the table could hear a massive sound like a rushing wind or the crash of a wave that encompassed the room, and as we all watched, we could see images like movies playing, which were the inside of my memories.

The first scene Jesus showed at the table was a time before my parents were divorced. My mother, brother, and I were waiting for my father to come up to the mountains and join us for Christmas. There had been a huge snowstorm, and we had been told that my father was unable to make it through the overwhelming amount of snow. We children just couldn't wait for him to get there—it just wasn't family without him! What we didn't know until later was that while we were waiting in great excitement and anticipation for our dad, he was spending time with Carol.

The second scene Jesus showed was more difficult: I was sitting at the top of the stairs overhearing a conversation my mother was having with a "lady friend" of my dad's. She was explaining to my mom that my father was with Carol at a party. This woman had also had an affair with my dad. I could hear my mother's cries, and it was almost unbearable for a twelve-year-old to hear. This was my introduction to the new persona of my father.

The third memory Jesus unfolded to those at the dinner table had taken place in our living room. I was trying to comfort my little brother's sobs as we had just learned that our father was leaving us. I looked up and saw my dad and mom come out of a closed room. My dad had a large picture of Carol in his hand. As they were walking out of the room, he said, "Does that make this any easier?"—referring to my mother being able to now put a face with Carol's name.

Jesus revealed the truth to this group at the dinner table without saying a word:

Why were these two young ones quiet and awkward in this social situation? Wouldn't you be?

Then, as I continued reflecting on this truthful picture, the dinner table changed and became a Communion table similar to the artist's rendering of the famous painting of the Last Supper that is so familiar. Jesus was in the center, serving the

Communion; my brother and I were on one side, and Carol, her family, and my father were on the other. Jesus then sat down and very soberly said, "One of you has betrayed me."

I leaned over and said, "Lord! Who is it? Is it me?" (I always blamed myself for everything.)

My dad spoke up and said, "Surely not I, Lord!"

The Lord answered my dad, "Yes, it is you!"

Then Jesus stood up again, and out of nowhere, he pulled out a chain saw! Everyone was alarmed, but my brother and I just looked at each other with big smiles of anticipation. What was he going to do now? All at once, Jesus raised the squealing chain saw in the air, and with one deliberate motion, bore down on the heavy table and sawed it right in half. My brother and I and Jesus were separated from the rest of the people.

But we were safe at Jesus' table.

And then, as I watched, before my very eyes, the table where we were sitting was transformed into the most exquisite table I had ever seen. In the center was a large round bowl filled with luscious fruit! Jesus' whole demeanor changed.

He picked up a great big juicy pear and exclaimed, "Oh! You gotta try this! It's joy!" We took great big hearty bites of the pear, and as we did, we all began to laugh out loud!

Then he grabbed another piece of fruit and said, "Take a piece of peace!" As we devoured the fruit, a deep peace settled over us, even in the presence of our enemies. Then, with an almost reverent tone, he said, "And now, the very best one! Take a bite of love!" As I bit down into the fruit, the juice ran down my face. Jesus laughed and said with great anticipation, "How did you like that?"

My heart was overflowing!

Now, filled with his love, I looked around the room and asked, "Jesus, where's my dad?"

With a sparkle in his eye, Jesus nodded his head toward the corner of the room. There, on the floor, was my father, weeping at the feet of Jesus. Jesus was at the table with me, but he was also right there, on the floor, with my dad.

He tenderly lifted my father's fallen face and spoke kindly to him: "You don't have to carry this any longer. I've already taken care of it."

As he spoke, Jesus pointed up to a mountainside. The room opened up and we could see the side of a mountain. On the mountain was a cross. And on the cross was a man.

What a beautiful picture!

My friend has relayed to me how meditative prayer has completely changed her life. When she saw Jesus rise up in righteous anger in defense of her and her brother, she told me she began to experience a boldness and confidence she had never before had. This has affected every area of her life, especially her ability to feel comfortable and confident in her day-to-day professional dealings with men. The image of Jesus' righteous anger has set her free from intimidation and feelings of awkwardness or being "on the outside."

One thing that is so wonderful about Jesus is that his righteous anger and his kindness go hand in hand for the purpose of redemption, and both are motivated by unconditional love.

YOUR PICTURE PRAYER EXERCISE

Sit quietly and ask yourself: *What am I feeling right now?* Look deeply below the surface to see if you are feeling angry about something. If so, allow yourself to acknowledge the anger. Visualize the situation that is bothering you—see the picture of the events unfolding.

Now take yourself out of the picture for a moment and try to view the situation objectively, as if you were a third party. Is your anger justified? Were you or someone you love wronged? Take a moment to visualize yourself doing what Jesus did on the cross. Visualize yourself saying, "Father, forgive them, for they don't know what they are doing." Let the bitterness go—God is the judge. Give them over into God's hands to do as he desires.

Now take a moment after you forgive them to acknowledge that in your righteous anger, it may be appropriate to "shake the dust off your feet" (Mark 6:11, NIV). Explore this option and ask the Holy Spirit to direct you. Recall your original picture and envision yourself "shaking the dust off your feet." Acknowledge that you can have a justifiable anger not rooted in bitterness, stress, or any other negative emotion but rooted in righteousness for the purpose of helping and protecting.

STATEMENTS TO PONDER

God is not afraid of my anger. He can handle it.

The price of "peace at all costs" is too high. I can be healthy and acknowledge my anger.

If I want to live in harmony with myself and with God, I must acknowledge that some people do not want that harmony as a goal.

I can be angry but not sin.

I can be at peace with God, although others disagree with me.

SCRIPTURES TO PONDER

Be angry, and yet do not sin. (Ephesians 4:26, NASB)

If any place will not welcome you or listen to you,

leave that place and shake the dust off your feet as a testimony against them. (Mark 6:11, NIV)

Do not give dogs what is sacred; do not throw your pearls to pigs. If you do, they may trample them under their feet, and turn and tear you to pieces. (Matthew 7:6, NIV)

CHAPTER 10

PERFECT LIE NUMBER SEVEN: I AM BAD

I MUST BE PERFECT BECAUSE MY ACTIONS DEFINE WHO I AM.

I will glory in the power of the cross,
And I will always give my life to one who didn't count it loss.
My accomplishments are not enough to cover up my sin.
The only way to be restored is just to let you in.

Fill my life, flood my soul,
Change my heart, make me whole.

JENNIFER CROW, "THE CROSS CANNOT FAIL," 2006

A FEW YEARS after its launch, Victory Church had assembled an outstanding, committed worship team. When Mark decided to add a Saturday night service, I realized that we could not expect the same volunteers to serve three times a week. Although the worship team members all seemed to want to participate in the third service, I believed the burden and commitment on each of them would become too much. I also reasoned it was a good time to invite people who had

171

recently joined our church and were musically talented to audition for the worship team.

My idea was to take the existing, experienced team and divide it into two groups. After holding auditions, we'd recruit new team members to fill in the gaps. That way we wouldn't be left with one experienced team and one inexperienced team to serve at all of our weekly services. Sounds logical, right?

Well, other than the new recruits and me, no one seemed to relish this idea. Still, I moved forward and found some wonderful new musicians (some of whom are still on our team today) and integrated them into the two teams. The latest musicians blended perfectly with the ones who had been there longer, but man, did I receive flack over the creation of two teams! People went so far as to tell me that they could no longer enjoy church because I had broken up the original group. I could not cause them to understand that we were welcoming *new* members who could become just as intimate with us as we had all become to one another—that we just needed to give the innovative plan a chance and some time.

Coincidentally, during that same period I asked the drummers to begin to utilize an in-ear metronome to set the tempo for each song. I hoped this would prevent the tempo from lagging or speeding up, which could make for some awkward moments during worship. What seemed to me like another simple fix resulted in a second firestorm. Among other things, some of the musicians complained that having the click in their ear from the metronome took away the extemporaneous "flow" of the worship experience.

Soon people began complaining, and some of their comments reached my husband. I tried to reassure Mark that I had everything under control. I was certain that once everyone became accustomed to the new plan, the dust would settle and everything would be *just fine*. Then, one by one, several of the worship team members began leaving the church. That had certainly not been my goal. Finally, my poor husband had had enough and called a meeting with two staff members and me. In the meeting, he made it clear that he did not want to cause any more disturbances to the team and we were going to have to stop using the metronome. Any benefit we gained from it, he said, wasn't worth its ramifications.

As he spoke, my mind was reeling. First, my husband was reprimanding me in front of other staff members. I wanted to act like a mature professional, but my emotions got the best of me and I started crying. Second, I knew that the metronome was *not* the issue and we needed to make this change to keep our music ministry moving forward. I was so angry that Mark seemed to be caving in to the whiners instead of looking at the bigger picture of what was best for the entire church.

I was so upset I couldn't think straight or get control of myself. To keep from making a bigger scene, I left the meeting and went out to my car, where I began sobbing. I drove out to a nearby lake and tried to calm myself down, but I just kept crying. I felt like I could not go on. When I started having trouble with my breathing, I instinctively began driving back toward the church. I could hardly see the road in front of me, I was crying so hard.

Once I had pulled into the back parking lot, I began hyperventilating. I didn't know what else to do, so I called my husband. How embarrassing that I couldn't get control of myself. My husband called our doctor, who said I was having a panic attack. Unfortunately, it was the first of many such attacks before the day I completely broke down in front of my suitcase.

It wasn't until I learned meditative prayer that I found healing and truly began to realize what had happened during that period of my life. I was unaware of the vicious diatribe of lies that was circulating with a vengeance through my neuropathways and upsetting the chemical balance of my body and nervous system. Only later did I realize that the most disturbing lie during that episode was the accusatory "You are *bad*," "You are *bad*," "You are *bad*." Alternate versions were "You are wrong"; "You messed up"; "You are a disappointment."

A person's system can only take so much of that negativity before he or she breaks, whether physically or mentally. Perhaps, like me, you have to go way back in time to remember the first time you told yourself, "I am bad."

I remember feeling like I was a bad little girl when I was about eight years old and out riding my bike. I had occasionally gotten in trouble before, but how much trouble can you really get into before the age of eight? As I was riding, a cussword popped into my mind. And then another one—and then a few more. And suddenly I felt so guilty I could hardly stand it! I remember feeling the weight of that sin—even as small as it was and as young as I was—bearing down on me. I was bad! Me—sweet, little Jennifer—had just thought some terrible words in my mind. What if I couldn't be forgiven? What if I was destined to be "bad" the rest of my life?

Maybe you can remember your first experience with guilt too. From the time each of us is born, the sin nature, which all human beings have inherited from Adam and Eve, tries to control our lives. No one really has to tell us that we are bad—we often know it down deep inside of ourselves.

Unfortunately, the feelings that we have about ourselves are often unwittingly confirmed by parents and teachers, even those who are truly loving. Because we value their opinions so much, their words have a tremendous impact. When you were a child and did something wrong, you may have immediately known you were in trouble, but when your mom or dad or your teacher yelled at you or punished you, it confirmed it! And if you had a parent or teacher who regularly lost his or her cool and became excessively angry over minor incidents, that self-awareness was sealed in the form of this lie:

I must be perfect because my actions define who I am.

If you believe this untruth, you probably have a hard time sorting out the difference between *you* and *your behavior*. And there is a big difference! The Bible tells us over and over again that God hates sin, but he *loves* the sinner. And because

Jesus died on the cross and paid the penalty for your sins, God no longer counts those sins against you. When you trust in Jesus as your Savior and accept the forgiveness God offers, you are no longer bad—not in God's sight, and hopefully not in your own sight, either.

Almost all of us carry some measure of guilt from "bad things" we've done: premarital sex, adultery, drinking, or so-called lesser sins like gossiping, telling a white lie, or feeling prideful or self-righteous. This guilt and shame can pile up and create a barricade that keeps us feeling separated from God.

Have any of the statements below ever been directed at you—whether by your parents, teachers, or even yourself?

"You are always getting into trouble."
"You are the black sheep of the family!"
"Why do you keep messing up?"
"What have you done now?"

If these statements echo words you have heard in the past, or even recently, you may notice the following feelings accompanying those thoughts:

Emotions associated with this lie
- *guilt*
- *shame*
- *fear of being found out*

LIE DETECTOR TEST

Ask yourself the following questions to determine if you believe the Perfect Lie: *I must be perfect because my actions define who I am.*

- Are there any patterns of addiction in your life (e.g., smoking, drinking, sexual addiction)? If you have habits you just can't break, you may have an image of yourself as being "bad." Until you can reprogram your mind and begin to see yourself as God sees you, the addictions may be difficult to overcome.
- Do you ever feel you have committed the "unpardonable sin"?
- Do you think of yourself as less worthy than other people to receive the love and forgiveness of God? To receive his blessings?

Our biggest mistake when dealing with this guilt is trying to handle it on our own—usually by trying to hide what we've done wrong. Scripture points to a better way, one which will permanently wipe away our sin. In fact, Romans 3:21-26 is one of my favorite passages because it gets to the heart of the matter. It shows us the better way God wants us to live:

Now God has shown us a different way of being right in his sight—not by obeying the law but by the way promised in the Scriptures long ago. We are made right in God's sight when we trust in Jesus Christ to take away our sins. And we all can be saved in this same way, no matter who we are or what we have done.

For all have sinned; all fall short of God's glorious standard. Yet now God in his gracious kindness declares us not guilty. He has done this through Christ Jesus, who has freed us by taking away our sins. For God sent Jesus to take the punishment for our sins and to satisfy God's anger against us. We are made right with God when we believe that Jesus shed his blood, sacrificing his life for us. God was being entirely fair and just when he did not punish those who sinned in former times. And he is entirely fair and just in this present time when he declares sinners to be right in his sight because they believe in Jesus.

The apostle Paul acknowledges that all of us fall short of God's standard. As Christ-followers, we long to have a vibrant, loving, personal relationship with the God of the universe. But we often go about it all wrong! We try to get to God by the things we do: by obeying our parents, by going to church, or by doing good deeds. But that won't get us where we so long to be. None of us can live up to his requirement of perfection.

After that horrible news, Paul reveals the stunning truth: Jesus "[took] the punishment for our sins . . . to satisfy God's anger against us." And now God can legally, righteously, and without compromising his own nature declare us "not guilty"! God knows that you are only human, that you will not reach perfection this side of heaven. But when you come to him, just as you are, he will clean you up, set you back on your feet, and speak to your heart: I love you. You are not bad! Instead, you're clean and pure and holy in my eyes.

Let that truth sink down deep into your spirit: You are not bad! You are free! You have been washed clean. As long as we walk this earth, we will continue to sin, even after God has begun transforming our lives. We don't have to beat ourselves up about it. We don't have to wallow in the guilt and the shame, because Jesus has already taken care of it. We can simply come to God and say, "Father, I confess my sin. Thank you that you have forgiven me for that stupid thing I just said. Thank you that you have forgiven me, and that I am not bad. I am righteous. I am pure and holy in your sight. Amen."

The Bible tells us that when we confess our sins, God is faithful and just to forgive those sins (see 1 John 1:9). He's done everything that needs to be done for us, everything that we couldn't do ourselves. All we have to do is accept it and thank him for it!

If there is something in your past that you are convinced can never be forgiven, notice that *you* aren't the faithful one in that verse—*Christ* is! In other words, no matter how "big" the sin, it is never bigger than God's grace and faithfulness. Author Lee Strobel, who once served as a teaching pastor at

Willow Creek Community Church near Chicago, explains how one woman was finally able to grab hold of this truth:

> We were doing a baptism service. We told people before they came up to the platform to be baptized to take a piece of paper, write down a few of the sins they'd committed, and fold the paper. When they came up to the platform, there was a large wooden cross on the stage. Each person was to bring that piece of paper, take a pin, and fasten it to the cross, because the Bible says our sins are nailed to the cross with Jesus Christ, and fully paid for by his death. Then they were to turn and come over to the pastor to be baptized.
>
> I want to read you a letter a woman wrote who was baptized in one of those services. She said: "I remember my fear. In fact, it was the most fear I remember in my life. I wrote as tiny as I could on that piece of paper the word *abortion*. I was so scared someone would open the paper and read it and find out it was me. I wanted to get up and walk out of the auditorium during the service, the guilt and fear were that strong.
>
> "When my turn came, I walked toward the cross, and I pinned the paper there. I was directed to a pastor to be baptized. He looked me straight in the eyes, and I thought for sure that he was going to read this terrible secret I had kept from everybody for

so long. But instead, I felt like God was telling me, *I love you. It's okay. You've been forgiven.* I felt so much love for me, a terrible sinner. It's the first time I ever really felt forgiveness and unconditional love. It was unbelievable, indescribable."

Do you have inside of you a secret sin that you wouldn't even want to write down on a piece of paper out of fear somebody might open it up and find out? Let me tell you something about the Jesus I know. Not only does he want to adopt you as his child, but also he wants to lift the weight of guilt off of your shoulders.[11]

God's love for you is overwhelming—it's so far beyond anything you could ever imagine. The Bible says that however high the heavens go, that's how great his love is for his children. Where do the heavens stop? The truth is, they don't! God's love is infinite—and he has removed your sins as far from you as the east is from the west. When the devil tempts you to believe the dirty lie that "you are bad," remind him (and yourself) of these facts:

God is sheer mercy and grace;
 not easily angered, he's rich in love.
He doesn't endlessly nag and scold,
 nor hold grudges forever.
He doesn't treat us as our sins deserve,
 nor pay us back in full for our wrongs.

As high as heaven is over the earth,
    so strong is his love to those who fear him.
And as far as sunrise is from sunset,
    he has separated us from our sins.
As parents feel for their children,
    God feels for those who fear him.
He knows us inside and out,
    keeps in mind that we're made of mud.
      (Psalm 103:8-14, THE MESSAGE)

ANTIDOTE TO THE SEVENTH PERFECT LIE

As a child, I learned that Christ forgives me and that his blood washes me clean. In fact, I can still recite the Prayer of Humble Access, a prayer I learned as a child during the Communion service at the Methodist church I attended as a child. It reads, in part:

We do not presume to come to this thy Table, O merciful Lord, trusting in our own righteousness, but in thy manifold and great mercies. We are not worthy so much as to gather up the crumbs under thy Table. But thou art the same Lord, whose property is always to have mercy: Grant us therefore, gracious Lord, so to eat the flesh of thy dear Son Jesus Christ, and to drink his blood, that our sinful bodies may be made clean by his body, and our souls washed through his most precious blood, and that we may evermore dwell in him, and he in us. Amen.[12]

I memorized the entire prayer after repeating it often, and while I enjoyed reciting and thought I believed the words, on another level my mind responded subconsciously to the negative thought patterns ingrained in my sin nature. The part about not being worthy to eat the crumbs under God's table really stuck with me. Rather than living in light of God's grace, I continued telling myself, *I am bad*.

The antidote to that lie came from purposefully thinking and meditating on 1 John 1:9, a verse we looked at earlier:

> If we confess our sins to him, he is faithful and just to forgive us our sins and to cleanse us from all wickedness.

Perhaps you've read this verse many times; perhaps you've even memorized it. This time, as you read it, try to picture the truth of this Scripture coming alive for you personally. What would it look like? When I think of myself confessing my sins to God, I remember another day when I was about eight years old and needed to confess something to my earthly father.

When my dad came home and changed after work, he always emptied his pockets and put his spare change on top of his dresser, which was just about at eye level for me. I was fascinated by how coins looked and felt, so I always noticed what he had left on his dresser. On this particular day I thought about how I could buy a piece of gum for a penny and three pieces of penny candy for a nickel. Boy, those coins looked especially appealing that day!

When no one was looking, I swiftly grabbed a nickel from my dad's dresser and hid it in my pocket. Later at supper, my dad seemed to look at me real funny, but he didn't say a word. That nickel seemed to burn a hole in my pocket as we cleaned up after dinner. Still, my dad never mentioned the missing nickel. Finally it was bedtime. I concealed that nickel in my closet. After reading us a story, my dad tucked my brother and me into our own beds. Lying in the dark, I tossed and turned and thought about that nickel. Finally, I couldn't stand it any longer!

I snuck out of bed, retrieved that nickel, and walked down the long, dark hall to the living room where my mom was watching TV and my dad was reading the paper. As I began to cry, my parents leaned forward in concern. I held out my sweaty little hand toward my dad and said, "Daddy, I stole your nickel off the dresser and I'm sorry!" As he reached his arm around me and took the nickel, I could tell that he wanted to smile, but he was trying to show the appropriate seriousness to go with my tears. He was so gentle and said, "Honey, I'm just glad you had the character to tell me. I hadn't even noticed. It's okay; I love you."

When I think of how God personally responds to me when I confess my sins, I believe he is at least as kind as my dad. So when I meditate on 1 John 1:9, I think of God my Father putting his arms around me, holding me close, and saying, "It's okay; I love you." His embrace swallows my pain; his love and cleansing forgiveness flow from his body to mine, filling every dark corner of my body, soul, and mind with his light. I meditate on this Scripture with my own hands touching my face or head and letting those hands be the conduit of Christ's healing, cleansing power into my very soul.

MY PICTURE PRAYER EXPERIENCE

A huge breakthrough for me came when I finally received a life-changing revelation of God's grace toward me. I was just a few weeks into my practice of prayerful meditation when I began each prayer session by asking myself, *Jennifer, what are you feeling right now?* Or *What lies are you believing?*

On this particular day, I was feeling that I was bad, not good enough. I asked myself another question that my counselor had taught me to ask: *When was the first time you can ever remember feeling this emotion?*

As I considered the tattered (mostly black-and-white—this was the sixties!) images from my early childhood, my mind settled on a day when I was about six. Like most moms, my mother liked things to be neat and in order. My brother (who was four) and I did not always follow her example.

My brother and I were playing in his room, which is where all the fun toys were. My mom came in and told us to clean up our toys by a certain time or we would be in trouble. She checked back with us a couple of times and sternly warned us that our time was almost up. She then tried to motivate us further by threatening to spank us if we didn't obey.

Toys were strewn everywhere. I heard her warnings, and I certainly didn't want a spanking, yet in my mind cleaning everything up seemed like an insurmountable task—not to mention that it was a lot more fun just to keep playing.

Finally my mom had had enough. Time was up. Fuming, she came into the room holding one of my daddy's leather belts. She pointed out that we had not done one thing to start cleaning up that room. She had warned us, she said. In my mind, I remember thinking, *Why didn't I listen to my mother? Why didn't I do what she said? I am a bad, bad girl, and now I will have to be punished!*

As I recall, my mom had my brother and me both lie across the bed on our stomachs while she hit us with an angry tirade of words and that belt. I remember thinking, *I deserve this—she warned me. I am a bad girl, and now I am getting what bad girls deserve.* I also said to myself something along the lines of: *Jennifer, you will never, ever let this happen again. Even though you are a bad girl, you will try to be so good that your mother will love you.*

My point in telling this story is not to judge my mom. I'd guess a similar scenario is repeated many times a day in households all over the world. I know that, unfortunately, I have disciplined my own children out of anger. Since I was a child at the time, I can't really say whether my mother was motivated by frustration or was simply displaying righteous anger when she spanked us. I do know that overall my mom was loving and wise. I love her very much, and I am so grateful for her leadership and wisdom in my life.

The point is that most of us have pictures in our minds from our past that stand as false evidence that *we are guilty and not worthy of love*. We deal with that guilt in different ways. Some people give up and follow their sin nature without a thought. In my case, I tried to be perfect. But I was still left with a sin consciousness that permeated the very fiber of who I thought I was. Whenever I thought back on that spanking, I felt very sad and very bad about myself.

Now, as I thought of that picture again during my prayer time, I prayed, *Holy Spirit, please show me a picture of the truth that was happening in that situation. Show me the antidote to the lie I have believed.*

I thought, *Well . . . I really was bad—I disobeyed my mother and reaped the consequences. Where's the lie in that?* I began to think of scenarios that might represent the truth of what happened. Would Jesus have rescued me from my mother before she ever spanked us? No, that didn't seem right—I had done wrong, and he wouldn't condone that. But what had he come to earth to do?

Then it dawned on me. As a picture of the cross and Jesus' crucifixion flashed before my mind's eye, the inspiration for a truthful picture began to unfold in my thoughts. In this new picture, I saw the same cast of characters, with a few additions.

As my mother spanked my brother and me and we cried,

I saw Jesus Christ enter the room. As I lay there on that bed, he fearlessly put his body in the path of the belt between my mother and me. He shielded me and pulled me away to the side, where my Father God was standing in the corner, waiting to envelop me in his arms with comfort and love.

As I watched Jesus take my place, I saw the anger and frustration in my mom's face. It dawned on me that my mother had her own stresses and difficulties in life at that time. She had had a difficult childhood. I realized she was hurting and was as much a victim of sin in this situation as I was. The Holy Spirit came in behind my mother and pulled her backward into his arms to comfort her. As she cried, he whispered, *I know what you are feeling. It's okay. Let me love you.*

As I stood with my Father God, I noticed that I, too, had changed. No longer was I a dirty-faced, barefoot child with matted hair; I was a beautiful young woman dressed in white. My hands were raised in praise to God. I was beautiful, nothing like the little girl with "grandma beads" around her neck (that's the Southern phrase for the little rings of dirt that collect in the tiny folds of the neck of a small child who has been playing out in the humid dirt of South Texas).

As I saw this picture of my redemption, I realized that I was not who I had thought I was all these years. I had a flash of revelation that told me the truth about myself—Jesus had taken my punishment for me, and since that time, God had never seen me as an outcast, but he had always seen me as I truly was—his child, his daughter, his princess. I was beautiful. And my desire was to serve him and to dedicate all my life to loving him and knowing him.

This new picture could supersede the old one. Even now, whenever I reflect on that day in my brother's room, I smile. I no longer feel bad or grieved, because I can see that situation truthfully, as it really happened: God loves me so much that he sent Christ to pay the penalty for my sin so that I can be his daughter and have right standing with him.

This meditative prayer enabled me to "renew my mind"; that is, wash my thoughts with the Word of God. I actually changed my view of my history to reflect an accurate portrayal of what happened.

YOUR PICTURE PRAYER EXERCISE

What is the worst thing you have ever done—that sin hidden away in the deepest, darkest part of you, the one that causes you the most guilt? When was the first time you can remember feeling guilty? Take some time in meditation to find a truthful picture about the situation.

Where was Jesus, and what was he doing? Perhaps picture your sin written on a piece of paper and then nailed to the cross of Christ. You have been forgiven! That sin is now as far from you as the east is from the west. Picture Jesus embracing you as you stand before him in pure white clothing—no guilt, no shame, only the freedom to bask in his glorious presence.

STATEMENTS TO PONDER

The wrong that I have done does not define who I am.

I am not bad. I am free from guilt and shame! I have been washed clean, and I am beautiful, holy, and pure in God's sight.

Today I will start living free to make the right choices.

SCRIPTURES TO PONDER

[The Lord says,] "I—yes, I alone—will blot out your sins for my own sake and will never think of them again." (Isaiah 43:25)

God did not send His Son into the world to condemn the world, but that the world through Him might be saved. (John 3:17, NKJV)

Now there is no condemnation for those who belong to Christ Jesus. And because you belong to him, the power of the life-giving Spirit has freed you from the power of sin that leads to death. (Romans 8:1-2)

CHAPTER 11

PERFECT LIE NUMBER EIGHT: I AM IN DANGER

I MUST ALWAYS BE ON GUARD
BECAUSE TROUBLE IS ALL AROUND ME.

Your thoughts toward me a melody,
Strong and clear and reaching me.
Your grace toward me a harmony,
Sustaining all my hopes and dreams.
Your love toward me a symphony,
Unyielding power taking over me.
You're all I want.
You're all I need.

JENNIFER CROW, "HIGHEST PRAISE," 2005

WHEN I WAS at my lowest point a number of years ago, I felt deep in my subconscious mind that life was so overwhelming I couldn't continue on. I would not say I was suicidal because I never would have considered taking my life. I have to tell you, though, that at times I just wanted to die and go be with God so I would not have to suffer any more pain.

191

I think what hurt most was the feeling that I didn't fit in or wasn't accepted by others. What's crazy is that if you had been looking in from the outside as an impartial observer of my life, you would think that I did fit in and that I was accepted. In fact, I probably looked like *the standard* of what it means to be accepted because I seemed to have many close relationships with family and friends. Inside, however, I was deeply sad and lonely, and I was just going through the motions much of the time due to the deceitful thoughts embedded deep in my brain.

Back when my children were babies, toddlers, and elementary-school aged, I homeschooled them, which helped me feel closely connected to them. But when the older four kids became teenagers, they were more independent and open about expressing their own views of life—which is just as it should have been. However, as the conflicts within our family increased, I took that to mean I wasn't enough, that I was a failure, that I wasn't loved for who I was, and that I didn't belong.

In my damaged way of thinking, I felt there were no longer any loving connections in my life (except perhaps with four-year-old Victoria, who brought some joy into my life—but then she had to love me because I was her mommy). I didn't feel loved and appreciated for who I was, but only for what I could do for others. I felt judged and criticized by my family members, coworkers, and members of our congregation just about every day. I felt I was letting my friends down, and I assumed they were nice to me only because they had to be.

I'm not saying my feelings and beliefs were accurate; I'm just expressing what I felt down in my soul. I would never have been able to verbalize all of this at the time. My thinking was so messed up I probably would have even denied these feelings. When your brain is wired a certain way, you begin to think that life as you know it is the norm. You know the old illustration of the frog that is put in a container of cold water and has a great ole time swimming around? When the pot he is swimming in is put on the stove, he doesn't feel it getting warmer and warmer. Because the water heats so gradually, he just keeps swimming and is cooked alive without ever realizing what happened. Most of us live our lives that way; we can't see objectively what we might easily see in the lives of others.

Throughout 2003, my feelings of danger centered around a nagging, torturous feeling that I did not belong and might be emotionally abandoned by those I loved. Then, because I did not think I could *live* without the love and emotional support of others, I was constantly striving to perform better and desperately searching for a way to alleviate conflict. However, my body and mind finally gave out when the level of pain and the energy I spent just trying to remain on guard got to be too much. I could no longer continue the charade that I was okay.

Perhaps your experiences haven't been as dramatic as mine. Or perhaps your feelings of danger come from another source. But all of us at one time or another will face this Perfect Lie, one of the most common and destructive lies that can infiltrate our minds:

I must always be on guard because trouble is all around me.

Emotions associated with this lie

- anxiety
- fear
- stress
- panic

As you may have figured out by now, my earliest memories involve fear—an immobilizing, paralyzing fear of being abandoned. I don't recall a time when my parents ever failed to meet my needs. They were not perfect, but they were certainly not abusive, and they provided a loving and stable home for me.

For some reason, however, I had several recurring abandonment nightmares that made me terrified of bedtime. In one of these dreams, my little brother and I were in a car that was parked at a gas station. My daddy had gotten out of the car to pump gas, but with just my brother and me inside, the car started moving—and no one was in the driver's seat. It may not sound that bad now, but to a little kid, it was absolutely terrifying.

I also had a recurring dream of being left alone on the beach with only a blue blanket.

In another nightmare, spacemen came into my attic from outer space and my parents were nowhere to be found. Enough already—you get the picture!

These nightmares turned into all kinds of other fears during the daylight hours. I was petrified of every kind of animal. When I was still a toddler, I decided to try to conquer this fear by sticking my finger through a neighbor's fence. I was promptly pecked by a rooster—the nip didn't even break the skin, but based on my reaction you would have thought I had been stabbed and was bleeding to death. That incident cemented into me a fear of animals that lasted for years.

I was also frightened of the shapes and images of monsters and glaring spacemen I saw in the wrinkles of the curtains in my bedroom. I was terrified by the sounds that emanated from my closet—even when I learned my parents had just been moving hangers around in their closet, which was adjacent to mine. We lived near a train track, and when I heard the whistle signaling an approaching train, I screamed in terror, fully believing that the locomotive was going to come off of its tracks and crash into my house. Obviously all these fears kept me hyperalert most of the time.

LIE DETECTOR TEST

How about you? Ask yourself the following questions to determine whether you also fall prey to the lie: *I must always be on guard because trouble is all around me.*

- Do you ever have recurring nightmares or awaken from sleep with a feeling of dread or darkness?
- Do you find yourself constantly making negative

statements about things that may or may not take place in the future?
- Do you exaggerate your own health problems or those of your family and friends?
- If you have a good day, do you wonder how long the "phase" will last?
- Are worry and fear a constant part of your life?

There is no doubt that most of the Perfect Lies that we struggle with become established in our thinking early in our lives. I am convinced that virtually every lie and wrong belief that takes root in our minds stems from a hurt that we were unable to interpret and cope with from a healthy perspective.

Unfortunately, once those false beliefs are planted and begin to grow in our mind, they are difficult to eradicate. I believe that's why, even after my family rededicated our lives to Christ when I was ten, my fears didn't all simply disappear. I now had a personal relationship with Christ and began to learn that I had a Companion closer than a brother who would never leave me. Yet it would be years—long after I was saved and Spirit-filled, with children of my own—before I realized how dreadfully filled with fear my thoughts had been for my entire life.

I am not saying that all fear is irrational. Fear, just like any of the other five basic human emotions of happiness, surprise, sadness, anger, and disgust, is neither good nor bad in and of itself. Fear at the most basic level is just a human emotion. It is helpful to have a healthy fear of jumping off the top of a three-story building. It is good to have a respectful fear of being disobedient to God so you are able to overcome your wrong desires and do what is right. And if a certain disease runs in your family, it is wise to consult with your doctor to make sure you remain healthy and take appropriate prevention measures. But fear that torments and prevents you and me from living with peace, faith, and courage is destructive. This kind of fear creates stress and begins to multiply, which leads to emotional, mental, and physical illness.

At the height of my illness and dysfunction, I became afraid of things that I had never been afraid of before, such as flying on an airplane, snow skiing, driving at night, driving in the rain, sleeping alone in the house, getting cancer, etc. I had never really enjoyed being up high, but now I became irrationally afraid of heights, to the extent that I abhorred even riding in an elevator.

Interestingly, studies show that most things we worry about—even when we aren't struggling with overwhelming fear as I was—never happen. One report states that the average person's anxiety is focused on:

things that will never happen: 40 percent

things about the past that can't be changed: 30 percent

criticism by others, most of which is untrue: 12 percent

their health (which, ironically, grows worse with stress and worry): 10 percent

real problems that might actually occur: 8 percent[13]

Of course, sometimes bad things *do* happen to good people. Everyone faces loss. One source of my irrational fears was my mistaken belief that my goal in life was to avoid all danger and prevent bad things from happening. Only then, I thought, would I be happy. But not only is it impossible to keep bad things from happening, it isn't even the right goal to have. Just consider what the Bible says about some of the unnamed heroes of the faith.

> [They] were tortured, refusing to turn from God in order to be set free. They placed their hope in a better life after the resurrection. Some were jeered at, and their backs were cut open with whips. Others were chained in prisons. Some died by stoning, some were sawed in half, and others were killed with the sword. Some went about wearing skins of sheep and goats, destitute and oppressed and mistreated. They were too good for this world, wandering over deserts and mountains, hiding in caves and holes in the ground. (Hebrews 11:35-38)

We often acknowledge the overcoming faith of the victors described in the first part of Hebrews 11 but skip over the uncomfortable details about the martyrs who refused to deny their Lord despite being subjected to horrendous pain and ridicule. Interestingly, the writer goes on to point out that none of them—neither the victors nor the martyrs—ever reached their goal here on earth. Verse 39 says, "*All* these people earned a good reputation because of their faith, yet none of them received all that God had promised" (italics added).

Despite the dangers we may face, God's Word is full of encouragement that we are not alone and that he never abandons us. If we choose to acknowledge our place as his beloved child, we belong to him. One of the best-loved promises from God to his children is found in Hebrews 13:5: "I will never fail you. I will never abandon you."

Since we can't experience him with any of our five senses, this can be a difficult truth to grasp. It doesn't always *seem* like he's with us. John 14:16-18 provides a bit more of an explanation:

> And I will ask the Father, and he will give you another Advocate, who will never leave you. He is the Holy Spirit, who leads into all truth. The world cannot receive him, because it isn't looking for him and doesn't recognize him. But you know him, because he lives with you now and later will be in you. No, I will not abandon you as orphans—I will come to you.

When Jesus left this world after his resurrection, he sent someone in his place who is actually the same spirit as God and Jesus—the Holy Spirit. The truth is we never walk alone through our troubles; God is with us through his Spirit.

How can that truth become real to us? For me, the answer is through meditative prayer, which helps my mind to find and adopt a truthful picture of God's constant presence. I was fortunate enough to have a dream one night a couple of years before I became so ill that illustrated the Scripture "I will never leave you nor forsake you" (Hebrews 13:5, NKJV). A part of that dream has formed a picture of truth in my mind that brings me comfort and assures me that I am not alone or abandoned.

In the dream, I was on the top of a beautifully scenic and gigantic mountain from which I could see fertile countryside for miles. Jesus Christ was with me in the flesh. He had the most penetrating eyes of love, and he was wearing a plaid flannel shirt, blue jeans, and hiking boots. As we hiked, his attention was completely on me. I could tell that he adored me, and I certainly adored him. He was such a gentleman, talking with me about things that concerned me and taking my arm to help me over the rough, rocky spots as we walked across the top of the lovely mountain ridge. We were having so much fun laughing and talking together that I almost didn't notice when we began a steep descent down the precipitous mountainside.

Before long, the path became narrower, but Jesus walked ahead of me to lead the way, always checking that I was safe and close behind him. I was completely unconcerned even as it dawned on me that the path on which we were walking was becoming downright treacherous! There was a steep cliff going up to my right, and straight down to my left was a cavernous, dangerous valley. The ledge I was walking on was barely wide enough for one person. But Jesus was in front of me, and he offered his hand to steady me as I carefully stepped down from rock to rock. His overwhelming care took my breath away. I realized just how special I was to him. I understood that I could not fall as long as he was beside me. We inched down into the valley that way for quite a while as the light became dimmer. The amazing thing that I noticed was that I did not feel *any* fear! In fact, my attention was so focused on my love for Jesus Christ and his love, care, and protection of me that I woke up feeling completely at peace.

In my darkest days, which were still to come, I hung on to the image of Jesus walking so closely with me. Yet I still feared so many things. Unfortunately, fear often comes in the form of a vague, unidentified sense that something bad is about to happen, that tragedy is just around the corner.

What I didn't yet realize was this: *The source of many of our fears is actually the fear of a loss.* Because I'd been so afraid of being abandoned—the ultimate loss—since I was a very young girl, I found myself bracing for anything that might broadside me and threaten me or my loved ones, whether loss of health, loss of property or finances, loss of prestige or security, or loss of love.

ANTIDOTE TO THE EIGHTH PERFECT LIE

One of Christianity's modern-day heroes of the faith is E. Stanley Jones, a longtime missionary to India and a close friend to and biographer of Mahatma Gandhi. He once wrote:

I am inwardly fashioned for faith, not for fear. Fear is not my native land; faith is. I am so made that worry and anxiety are sand in the machinery of life; faith is the oil. I live better by faith and confidence than by fear, doubt, and anxiety. In anxiety and worry, my being is gasping for breath—these are not my native air. But in faith and confidence, I breathe freely—these are my native air. . . . We are inwardly constructed in nerve and tissue, brain cell and soul, for faith and not for fear. God made us that way. To live by worry is to live against reality.[14]

Here is the truth that Jones knew, the truth that will combat this Perfect Lie: we have no reason to fear because God goes with us through every situation!

Earlier in this book, I shared with you one of my favorite parts of the Bible, Psalm 23, which I meditated on many nights when trying to fall asleep. Since I have discovered that the key to facing fear is the knowledge that I am not alone, not abandoned, this Scripture has helped me battle fear in my life. As a child, I heard it recited in the King James Version: "Yea, though I walk through the valley of the shadow of death, I will fear no evil: for thou art with me" (verse 4).

Upon hearing that verse, I was prone to focus on the scary "valley of the shadow of death" part (which in my mind was spoken by someone with a deep, scratchy voice, with the word *death* reverberating in an echo over and over). Who wanted to think about, much less talk about, *that* Scripture! I wanted to shove that thought to the back of my mind.

But after having the dream of Jesus walking with me down the treacherous side of that mountain into the deep, dark valley, I have a different opinion of that "valley of the shadow of death" experience. First of all, I like how the verse in the King James Version starts out: "YAY!"

I know the verse really reads "yea," but I like to think of it as "yay!" I can celebrate because Jesus is with me; he is touching me; he is holding me; he is paying personal, careful attention to me. His complete focus is on me right now.

If you have ever been in love, you know that feeling of overwhelming love and warmth down in your heart, when all you can think about is your loved one. That was the feeling that caused Mark, when we first met, to attend an opera with me instead of playing in a softball game. He just wanted to *be* with me no matter what the circumstances.

That is the way you are loved by Jesus, and that is the way you can love him. The Scriptures say that you are the apple of his eye; that your name is tattooed on his hands.[15] Even if you imagine yourself in a dangerous situation, picture Jesus right there with you—and notice how wonderful it is to be right beside him even then. As you picture you and Jesus loving each other this way, you will find that your physical body responds. Your body will relax as endorphins are released, and your stress will begin to melt away. Habitual reflection on such revolutionary but truthful pictures was key to my healing and the complete transformation of my mind.

You and I must gain a true and deep understanding of how much God loves us—letting it sink deep into our very souls, our emotions, the deepest part of our selves. And when that love penetrates our hearts, there is no fear that the devil can bring to torment us any longer.

You are loved. There is no reason to fear! You are not doomed—God has great plans for your life!

MY PICTURE PRAYER EXPERIENCE

During the first weeks of my sabbatical, the time I took away from everyone and everything so I could find healing, I was still very ill and fatigued, but I had begun to change the pictures in my heart through the exercise of meditative prayer. During the few hours I did sleep, I still had disturbing dreams, however. It was almost as if there was a battle going on inside my heart and my mind. Even though I was combating the lies by changing the pictures in my mind during my waking hours, my subconscious mind seemed to be fighting to keep me in torment throughout the night.

One morning I awoke from a particularly frightening dream. In the dream, I was asleep in the back of a motor home in which my husband, Mark, my children, and I were all traveling. The dream was nothing like the vacation we had actually taken one year, in which we accidentally went through the Holland Tunnel in Manhattan in a motor home. That experience was more of a comedy—but this dream was anything but funny.

The nightmare started out peacefully: I was dozing lazily, relaxing and enjoying the gentle hum of the tires rolling down the highway. I could hear the laughter of my children playing a board game in the back of the motor home with their dad. Wait a minute! With their *dad?* If Mark was in the back, then *who was driving the motor home?* I shot straight up like a rocket and stared, in horror, at the empty driver's seat as the motor home careened out of control.

At that point, I awoke in a panic—and with a strange sense of déjà vu. It dawned on me that this was very similar to the dream I'd had as a child, the one where my brother and I were in the car at the gas station with no one behind the wheel.

I hadn't thought about that dream in years, although it had been a weekly occurrence when I was young. Perhaps, I reasoned, there was significance to this dream suddenly appearing again, even though it was in a different form. Maybe God was trying to show me something.

I decided to try to change the nightmare and inject it with the truth of God's Word. What was the picture revealing to me? Why did I feel deserted by those who loved me? Why was I feeling so vulnerable and unprotected? How could my family put me in so much danger and yet be completely oblivious to what was happening? And where was God in all of this?

I tried changing the picture of my dream in my mind in several different ways. Should Mark come to the rescue and rush up to the driver's seat, take the wheel, and save the day? Nothing against my husband—he is a very fine man—but somehow that scenario didn't make me feel any better. Perhaps I should climb over the seat myself, grab the wheel, and get the vehicle back under control. No, I realized, that wouldn't work, either—especially in my childhood dream. There was no way I could get there in time, and as a four-year-old, I didn't even know how to drive.

Gradually, the answer began to develop. I realized that the driver's seat really wasn't empty, as it appeared to my fearful mind. Instead, the Holy Spirit was at the wheel, and he was calmly steering the car back under control. Just as he had been guiding my life all these years, he was in charge and watching out for my well-being, whether I noticed him in the driver's seat or not.

I began to picture the Holy Spirit in the front seat. He was happy, having a good old time driving along. With that image in mind, I saw myself relaxing, smiling, and going back to sleep in the back of the motor home, resting in the knowledge that God was in control of my life, my family, my husband, and my children. He was "driving" us exactly where we needed to go.

Carrie Underwood's popular song "Jesus, Take the Wheel" skyrocketed up the charts not too long ago. The reason this concept resonated with so many people is that all of us feel that our lives are unmanageable at times—and we need someone greater than us, stronger than us, to take the wheel and bring things back under control. Jesus is that someone, and that reality is not just a trivial hope expressed in a country song. If we give Jesus our fears and anxieties, he promises to give us a peace beyond all human understanding. We can relax in him and know that, no matter what happens, everything will be okay.

YOUR PICTURE PRAYER EXERCISE

Meditative prayer and Scripture reading helped me overcome my fear of abandonment. My soul was finally able to rest in the truth that *I am never truly alone*. Once I truly understood that I belong to God and am a part of his family, I had the power to face and overcome every other destructive fear in my life. When I added Jesus to the picture, every fearful situation became much less menacing.

During a quiet time of meditation, I recommend that you try to grasp this truth for yourself. First, ask what it is that you fear most. (An example for me might have been an airplane crashing with me in it—now there's a picture!) Allow yourself to picture this event taking place, but in the middle of your visualization, picture Jesus entering the scene and taking control. What difference does the powerful presence of Christ make in the situation?

Second, once you acknowledge and identify the fear, ask yourself: *What emotion am I feeling?* For example, you might be feeling panic, hysteria, uneasiness, etc.

Third, ask yourself, *When is the first time I can ever remember feeling this emotion?* I don't necessarily mean the literal situation that you are in right then, but the first time you felt the emotion, such as panic, for example.

Fourth, find the truth or the antidote to this lie and incorporate the truth into your picture so that the picture is changed. For example, I pictured a giant Jesus standing on earth holding the airplane like a toy and assisting it as it was flying. (You may think I'm crazy, but this kind of thinking changed my life and my health!)

Finally, think regularly about that new picture for the next several days or months. Before you know it, you will have built a new, truthful neuropathway that attracts like thoughts and begins to grow and develop positively. Soon that new picture will become more powerful and will replace the old picture as your default programming.

To completely derail that underlying fear, start the cycle again and ask yourself, *When was the next time I remember feeling "panicked"?* and continue on through the process.

Because of what God has done for us through Jesus, we do not have to put up with this lie any longer.

STATEMENTS TO PONDER

Because of God's perfect love penetrating my life, I have no reason to fear.

No matter what happens to me, the Lord will still be with me, and he has an amazing, incredible plan for my life.

I choose to focus my mind on the good things of God, not on Perfect Lies, for I have the spirit of love, power, and a sound mind.

I am not doomed—I am destined for great things, a life filled with righteousness, peace, and joy in the Holy Spirit.

SCRIPTURES TO PONDER

Even if my father and mother abandon me, the LORD will hold me close. (Psalm 27:10)

Don't love money; be satisfied with what you have. For God has said, "I will never fail you. I will never abandon you." (Hebrews 13:5)

Be sure of this: I am with you always, even to the end of the age. (Matthew 28:20)

Don't be afraid, for I am with you. Don't be discouraged, for I am your God. I will strengthen you and help you. I will hold you up with my victorious right hand. (Isaiah 41:10)

I called on your name, LORD, from deep within the pit. You heard me when I cried. . . . Yes, you came when I called; you told me, "Do not fear." (Lamentations 3:55-57)

God did not give us a spirit of timidity (of cowardice, of craven and cringing and fawning fear), but [He has given us a spirit] of power and of love and of calm and well-balanced mind and discipline and self-control. (2 Timothy 1:7, AMP)

CHAPTER 12

PERFECT LIE NUMBER NINE: I AM DEPRIVED

I MUST INDULGE MYSELF IN ORDER TO BE HAPPY.

I hold to this truth that will always remain,
A promise of life that can't be contained.
Though outwardly we are wasting away,
Our life is renewed every day.
We fix our eyes on what remains unseen, this vital truth.

CHRIS CROW AND JENNIFER CROW,
"HOLD TO THIS TRUTH," 2008

I AM AN IDEALIST, which means I have high standards and work hard to achieve my goals in life. On the downside, I often think where I am or what I have right now is not enough, that it is somehow "less than."

When I was single, I dreamed of the day when I would marry Prince Charming and all my feelings of loneliness would end. While lying in bed in my college dorm, I thought about how much better my life would be if only I could find that perfect guy. When it seemed I had found him, I was dismayed to discover that his only job was as a bagger at the grocery store down the street.

After Mark and I married, I continued dreaming of what life would be like when one of us finally found a job that paid enough so we could buy a house, furniture, and some pretty dishes (a particular favorite of mine). On my husband's first youth-pastor salary, we barely had enough to live on, much less save for a house or furniture. For years we moved from rental house to rental house, dragging along the hand-me-down furniture and dishes that had belonged to my grandmothers.

For a break from the daily stresses of my humble, meager life, I read decorating magazines, escaping for a time into a world of breathtaking show homes, unimaginably expensive and exquisite furniture, and designer sets of dishes for every occasion. I would view the colorful, glossy photographic spreads in those magazines and dream of the day when I might possibly be able to have even a tiny taste of that luxury and beauty. If only I could have those things, that house, those clothes, that car . . .

After four years of marriage, we seemed nowhere closer to getting those things. We were living in a two-bedroom duplex in Victoria, Texas, and Mark was making $16,000 a year, along with a $1,500 annual book allowance, from the church for which he worked. I was thinking, *Books! He doesn't need books; he needs furniture!* I don't remember exactly what our reasoning process was at the time, but I guess we decided,

Well, if we can't buy furniture, let's just have a baby, because Christopher was born while we were living in that duplex.

Then I fell into a new round of "if onlys." When my precious Christopher learned to sleep through the night, I thought, *If only my baby would learn to walk, then life wouldn't be so hard*. When he learned to walk, I thought, *If only my baby were school age, then life wouldn't be so hard*. I lived in an imaginary future world where everything was wonderful as compared to my life in the here and now, which was definitely less than wonderful.

This was a lie I believed in every area of life, from vacations, which were nonexistent (except for the trips to visit my folks in Texas, who thankfully treated us as if we were staying in a fancy hotel), to clothing for me and my family, which was either secondhand or purchased at a budget store. I felt deprived compared to everyone else I knew, including my brothers, in-laws, other family members, and close friends. That feeling of deprivation could at times turn into desperation as I lay in bed at night thinking about all I wanted but didn't have. I would try to count my blessings. I knew I should be grateful for what I had, but I just couldn't kick the feeling that something was missing in my life.

Then I began to observe something interesting. Even when Mark and I began reaching some of our goals, the nagging feeling of deprivation did not go away! After ten years of marriage and four children, our good friend, pastor, and employer Jim Graff recommended that Mark receive a bonus that enabled us to put a down payment on a home.

We were thrilled, but once we had purchased our fixer-upper home, the "if only" cycle began yet again. *If only we could get new carpet, then life wouldn't be so hard. If only we could have a bigger closet, then life wouldn't be so hard.* I think you get the picture.

Several years after we moved to Oklahoma City and planted Victory Church, I became pregnant with my fifth child, little Victoria, and we moved to a larger house to make room for her. By that time, the church had grown and the house we were able to afford was like a dream home compared to the rental houses we had lived in for the first few years of our marriage. We also finally had the resources to buy some furniture and have some intentional (not accidental) decorating.

But along with the blessing came a desire for more: *If only we had a pool, then we could have great family time, and life wouldn't be so hard. If only we had a guest bedroom, then life wouldn't be so hard.* Even then, when we were so blessed as compared to eighteen years earlier, I always seemed to feel deprived. I actually had the opposite problem from the apostle Paul, who said he had learned to be content in every situation.

I had learned to feel deprived in every situation!

This feeling that we're deprived often sneaks up gradually, without us even being aware of its approach. Several years ago author and college president Joe Stowell and his wife moved out of downtown Chicago to the western suburbs to be near their grandkids. They built what they considered their dream house. It was not over the top, but they liked how it looked from the curb and how it "lived" inside. Then about six months after they moved in, Joe was driving through another neighborhood when a house caught his attention. He was drawn by its colors, architecture, and location. And his first thought was, *Boy, do I wish I had that house!*

He compares his feelings that day to what Eve must have gone through in the Garden:

Have you ever wondered, *What is wrong with us?* It's the Eve factor in our lives. We were born with it, and it's deeply embedded in our spiritual DNA. Just one more proof of our sinfulness, in case we had forgotten. What was it that drew Eve's heart away from God in Genesis 3? What was it that seduced her into the material world, into Satan's clutches? She wanted more. What she had, although awesome and satisfying, wasn't enough.[16]

For so many years, I was a bit like Eve, believing the devil's lie that what I had been given was not enough. I did not live my life in the present tense. I was always planning for the future, waiting on something new or exciting to happen to me that would make me happy, that would make me feel like my life was worthwhile.

This is the ninth Perfect Lie:

I must indulge myself in order to be happy.

The enemy would love nothing more than to blind us to the beauty and importance of the day we are living today. But so many people believe that we need something to change in our lives before we will be satisfied. In other words, we think, *I must have something more before I will be okay.*

Have you ever had any of these thoughts or made any of these statements out loud?

When I have a big house, then I'll be happy.
When I have a child, then I'll be happy.
When I get that prestigious job with a huge salary, then I'll be happy.

Or what about these:

I must have my prescription drugs or I won't be able to sleep at night.
I must have dessert at every meal or I just won't feel like I've really eaten.

These thoughts reflect the lie the devil told Eve in the Garden. He convinced her that her life wasn't satisfactory, that she needed something more in order to be happy and that God was holding out on her. She and Adam bought into the lie—and we do the same thing today. Ironically, dwelling on these kinds of thoughts often leads to more dissatisfaction and sadness.

Emotions associated with this lie

- *impatience*
- *anger*
- *frustration*
- *insecurity*
- *craving for love substitutes (addictions)*

According to a 2009 report in *Psychology Today*, four thousand books were published on the subject of finding happiness in 2008—up from just fifty books in 2000.[17] It seems we are obsessed with the pursuit of happiness—but are we searching in all the wrong places?

What is it that you think will make you happy? Something that you don't have right now, that you think "if only" you did have, your life would be perfect? We all find that our thinking sometimes gets in ruts that don't lead anywhere good. But these kinds of thoughts will put you in bondage faster than anything else. You will begin to miss out on the wonderful things in your life right now, *today*, if all you are doing is hoping for something better in the future. Whether it's an extra slice of cheesecake or a new pair of shoes, or something bigger like a new career, house, or husband, the truth is, you don't *have* to have these things in order to live a beautiful life of satisfaction and contentment.

LIE DETECTOR TEST

Do you ever find yourself mired in unhappiness because of what you don't have? Answer the questions below to see if you've fallen prey to the devil's Perfect Lie: *I must indulge myself in order to be happy.*

- Do you often find yourself telling yourself, *If only . . . then . . . ?*
- Do you find it hard to trust that God will provide all you need in life?
- Do you feel the need to make things happen yourself, instead of waiting patiently for God's timing?

There is no substitute for the love that only God can give. There is no substitute for receiving his blessings in his timing—which is always perfect. As long as you think, *Until I get this particular thing, I can't be okay*, you will be miserable.

You may be living this type of existence right now. I lived there, too, for many years. It wasn't until I was forty years old that it dawned on me that I needed to start enjoying my life right now, instead of thinking, *When the next great thing happens, then I'm going to be happy.* I have learned (finally!) that it doesn't work that way. All we really need is God's love—and that is something we already have.

God's love is shining down on you this very day, letting you know how wonderful you are and that you have everything you need to be okay. Let that truth sink in: God has provided everything that you need to be okay right now—*in this very moment.*

That word *contentment* is really the key. The emotions associated with this Perfect Lie are actually the opposite of contentment: they are impatience, anger, frustration, and insecurity! And that makes complete sense, if you think about it. If you are always hoping for something better, when that something doesn't come, you are very likely to get impatient—with God, with yourself, and with those around you. That leads to anger, frustration, and ultimately insecurity, especially if you feel that what you desire is actually essential for life to be worthwhile.

One of the most important verses in the Bible is one that I used to hate—but only because I misunderstood it. It says this:

> I have learned how to be content with whatever I
> have. I know how to live on almost nothing or with
> everything. I have learned the secret of living in
> every situation, whether it is with a full stomach or
> empty, with plenty or little. (Philippians 4:11-12)

The word *learned* there is so important! We have to learn how to be content with what we've been given. I have learned—and I'm still learning! I have to get up every day and in my time of meditative prayer (remember, these are small increments of time—five minutes or so) I ask myself, *What is the truth about me today? Am I okay in the midst of my current situation? Am I going to have a happy day today or not? Which way is my day going to go?* And you know, the answers to those questions are entirely up to me!

The apostle Paul shares with us a secret in this verse—the secret to "living in every situation," both good and bad. Actually, this is the secret that the world is constantly searching to find—the secret to happiness, the secret to feeling like a million bucks every single day of our lives. What is the secret? Paul tells us in the next verse: "I can do everything through Christ, who gives me strength" (Philippians 4:13).

Because we have Christ, we don't need anything else. I am okay right where I am, even in the midst of turmoil or adversity, because he is the One who gives me strength—not my own strength, but his: his strength of love, power, a sound mind, peace, joy, and faith. He gives all of that to you and me freely.

But how can you receive it? By meditating on the truth of who he is and what he thinks of you. By keeping his Word in your heart. When you live this way, it won't stress you out if you can't make your mortgage payment. It may be a challenge—but it is not a challenge that can't be overcome, and you can still have peace and joy in the situation. What if the unthinkable does happen and your lender kicks you out on the street? Well, then you can move in with family members. Your family can't or won't take you in? Well, then you can go to the City Rescue Mission. You will still be okay!

I don't want to make light of what has become a very

distressing situation for some families today, but at the same time, we need to remember Jesus' caution against worrying "about everyday life—whether you have enough food and drink, or enough clothes to wear. Isn't life more than food, and your body more than clothing? Look at the birds. They don't plant or harvest or store food in barns, for your heavenly Father feeds them. And aren't you far more valuable to him than they are?" (Matthew 6:25-26).

Whether we have little or much, just about everyone—with the possible exception of those living in third-world countries that have been struck by famine—will be able to find food and shelter. God will provide you with everything that you *need*—it may not always be what you *want* at the moment, but if you think about it, he's created a world that provides everything for you: human beings need air to breathe and water to drink, and it just so happens that the earth is filled with air and water. It's almost a no-brainer to live on this planet because by God's provision he shows how much he cares for his creation.

Too often we are like the little child who falls down and skins his knee. Ever notice that even if there is barely even a red mark, the child begins screaming as if he were dying? What do we say to the child? After hugging and comforting him, we encourage him by telling him, "It's all right. You're okay!" We see the situation from the more informed perspective of an adult who knows that the child is going to be fine. We see that this tiny little moment of pain is not going to last forever.

In the same way, we have a heavenly Father who knows that life will ultimately work out, and justice will be done even as our lives extend into eternity. With this understanding, I now sometimes speak to myself like I would to that toddler, saying, *You're okay. You're okay, Jennifer. You are going to be fine. God adores you just the way you are, and he is taking care of you.*

That is the power of the gospel of Jesus Christ—that he cares for you. If you have not yet partnered up with God your Creator, you need to do so! When you rely on him for your every need, you no longer have to worry about anything. No matter what happens, you will be okay because he is always with you.

ANTIDOTE TO THE NINTH PERFECT LIE

Shortly after I became a Christian at age twelve, I learned Matthew 6:34: "Don't worry about tomorrow." It's part of a well-known passage of Scripture:

> You cannot serve both God and money.
> That is why I tell you not to worry about everyday life—whether you have enough food and drink, or enough clothes to wear. Isn't life more than food, and your body more than clothing? Look at the birds. They don't plant or harvest or store food in barns, for your heavenly Father feeds them. And aren't you far more valuable to him than they

are? Can all your worries add a single moment to your life?

And why worry about your clothing? Look at the lilies of the field and how they grow. They don't work or make their clothing, yet Solomon in all his glory was not dressed as beautifully as they are. And if God cares so wonderfully for wildflowers that are here today and thrown into the fire tomorrow, he will certainly care for you. Why do you have so little faith?

So don't worry about these things, saying, "What will we eat? What will we drink? What will we wear?" These things dominate the thoughts of unbelievers, but your heavenly Father already knows all your needs. Seek the Kingdom of God above all else, and live righteously, and he will give you everything you need.

So don't worry about tomorrow, for tomorrow will bring its own worries. Today's trouble is enough for today. (Matthew 6:24-34)

For years I read these verses and mentally agreed with all of these principles. I shouldn't worry about tomorrow. *Of course not! Why would I do that? God's got everything under control!*

But only when I began practicing prayerful meditation did I become mindful of my physical surroundings so that I could focus on the here and now and learn to live in each and every moment. In this instance, I did this by acknowledging my five senses and the truth about my surroundings.

As I read the words of Jesus, I saw that he encourages his followers to look at the world of nature to see the truth: we are not deprived in this world. He tells us to look at birds, flowers, and fields, and he tells us to observe how God provides for plants and animals at the most basic level.

So to overcome the lie "I must indulge myself in order to be happy," which stems from the lie that I can't be happy unless I have a perfect life, I sit and reflect as Jesus directs me to do, either outside in nature or while looking out a window on the world. Then I ask myself some questions:

Did the sun rise today? Yes.

Is it likely it will rise again tomorrow? Yes.

I observe the weather using my senses of sight, feeling, hearing, and smelling and ask:

Are the clouds and weather operating in a systematic, predictable way? Yes. (Well, since I live in Oklahoma, I guess I have to say, "Most of the time"!)

I take a deep breath in and a deep breath out. I gaze at God's world and ask:

Do I have oxygen today? Yes.

Is it likely I will have oxygen for the rest of the day? Yes.

I scan the sensory feelings inside and outside my body. I carefully observe any aches and pains or good feelings and ask:

Am I okay right now? Yes.

Do I need any physical thing to make me more comfortable?

If I need to, I adjust my clothing or sitting position to become as comfortable as possible.

Am I thirsty right now? Do I have access to clean water to drink? Yes.

Am I hungry today? Will I have food in my pantry or can I find food to eat today? Yes.

I observe my surroundings.

Am I safe? Is anyone trying to attack me or take my life? I am safe.

If I'm inside, I look at the roof over my head and ask:

Do I have a place to lay my head when I'm tired today? Yes.

Do I have clothes to wear today? Yes.

What I observe is that right now, I am perfectly fine. I have air, clean water, food, and shelter. When I think about a scenario in which I would *not* have those things, I realize that I am very far from that scenario in this moment. I remember that human beings existed for thousands of years without water purification systems and grocery stores, and yet humans have not been in danger of extinction for a long time, if ever. I realize that our heavenly Father, God, has put us in a world where we have what we need to survive. In this moment, I am safe, protected, at rest. I have everything I need.

I thank God for the roof over my head that protects me from the sun and rain. I am grateful for the fireplace in the winter and the cool breeze in the summer. I am thankful that chances are I will live to see the sun shine on another day.

Every time I meditate, I have learned to take a few

moments to observe what is around me, to go outside for a few moments, to look out the window and see that the world is continuing on regardless of and oblivious to my drama. I observe the steady provision of nature and realize, *I am not deprived.* This relieves me of the stress of wishful thinking and unfulfilled dreams, which can wreak havoc on mind, soul, and body. I realize instead the truth of Jesus' words: "Seek the Kingdom of God above all else, and live righteously, and he will give you everything you need" (Matthew 6:33).

MY PICTURE PRAYER EXPERIENCE

Just a few months after I began experiencing healing in my body and soul, Mark and I bought a 100-year-old farmhouse on a large piece of land. The lifeline connecting us to the outside world was a lonely, narrow, half-mile winding road through fields of hay from our house to the mailbox. I cannot tell you how many times I have poured out my heart to God while walking, jogging, or rollerblading that path. Many of the songs I've written were started or crafted on that road.

One late summer day when the fields were tall with unmowed grains that blew gently in the breeze, I was walking on the road and began thinking through what was on my mind that day. Then it occurred to me that I was always telling God what was on my mind. Why didn't I ever ask him what was on his mind? So I set aside my prayer requests and said out loud, "Lord, I'm always talking to you about what's on my mind; what's on your mind today?" Just as the question escaped my lips, I almost wished I hadn't asked. What serious world issues must God be facing today? Starving people in an African country? Numerous children being abused, nameless to me but known to him? I almost didn't want to know what he might be thinking about! Surely it would be too heavy, serious, and depressing for me to handle. And yet the question had already been asked. It was out there hanging . . . begging for a response.

As the sun beat down with only the sound of a dragonfly buzzing across the fields, I heard a voice in my mind say softly, *Jennifer, do you want to know what I am thinking about today?*

Another silent pause.

Again, I heard this still, small voice: *Look at the small stalk of grain that is growing on the side of the road. Didn't I create that beautifully? Look how intricate each tiny seed fits into a pattern on the head of the grain. Aren't my works spectacular? And look at the detail that I have put into every living thing that you can see. Look how the living things in my world interact with the things that are not alive, the rocks and the ground and the clouds and the weather. Jennifer, that is what I am thinking about today. I am thinking about and enjoying the beauty of the marvelous, perfect world I have made.*

I had the distinct impression that God was relishing his creation and inviting me to enjoy it with him! And as I noticed the wonderful details in each living thing I passed by day after day and never noticed, I began to brag on him too. I marveled at the tiny, humble grain grown to make hay for cows to eat. I marveled at how beautiful and amazing each stalk was and how perfectly it was placed in its environment.

As I began to notice and be in awe of each tiny detail, I felt that God and I were joining in a mutual admiration society concerning his amazing creation. We went on and on extolling the virtues of each bird, each tree, and each cloud. Then he stopped me short with one comment:

And Jennifer, when I created all of this . . . I had you in mind.

The tears began to fall as I realized that what God was thinking about that day and almost all the time was *me*. And that almost everything he did in this world was for *me* and because he loved *me*. I knew that I was not the center of the universe, but somehow I understood that I was in the center of his heart. God hadn't singled me out either; each person he created is just as special, just as loved. The personal experience I was having with him was available to anyone who dared ask God, *What are you thinking today?*

As I walked along, the words and melody began to form in my mind: "Every blade of grass I see, you created just for me. The world and all its majesty is crying out your love for me." Once I was back home, I went inside and sat down at my piano in the front parlor of our old house. I opened the notebook I keep on the piano and began to copy the words that were flowing from my heart.

Ironically, I'd spent much of my life waiting for the day when I'd have more time for songwriting. It was only when, in the midst of my imperfect life, I took the time to sit at

Jesus' feet and consider the blessings he'd provided all around me that I was able to begin writing songs for him that fill me with great joy—and remind me of all I have because of Christ's great love for me.

YOUR PICTURE PRAYER EXERCISE

Imagine a picture of yourself, completely loved and cared for in the midst of your current situation or weakness. What is the truth about God's love for you even if your situation *never* changes? Take a walk through your home, through your yard, or through your neighborhood, asking God to show you what he was thinking about as he created each living thing you see. Then thank him for placing you right where you are, in the middle of all these great gifts.

Beyond all the visible reminders of his care and concern, remember that nothing can take away his love for you—nothing! Knowing that truth makes the inconveniences of life—sickness, grief, poverty, and strife—lose their controlling power over your being. Live in the moment and enjoy God's love.

STATEMENTS TO PONDER

God, my heavenly Father, knows what I need even before I ask him.

My trust and hope is in God alone, who richly provides me with good things of every kind to enjoy.

I am more than just "okay"—I am a beloved and cherished child of God, fully whole and content with all the blessings that have been showered into my life.

SCRIPTURES TO PONDER

If we have enough food and clothing, let us be content. (1 Timothy 6:8)

Don't love money; be satisfied with what you have. For God has said, "I will never fail you. I will never abandon you." (Hebrews 13:5)

This same God who takes care of me will supply all your needs from his glorious riches, which have been given to us in Christ Jesus. (Philippians 4:19)

CHAPTER 13

QUESTIONS AND ANSWERS ABOUT CHRISTIAN MEDITATIVE PRAYER

WHEN PERFECT LIES are allowed to dominate our thoughts, they can stifle our faith, plague our minds, and even take a toll on our bodies. Unfortunately, they are not easy to eradicate. Willpower and good intentions did not cure me. The remedy that does break down these lies, I discovered, is meditative prayer. Without it, I'm not sure I would have ever recovered from the poisonous thoughts and debilitating physical symptoms I was experiencing.

Throughout this book, I have encouraged you to practice visualizing Jesus coming into the pictures in your mind to combat the lies that have tormented you and to allow him to change those pictures and set you free. (The truth will always set you free! See John 8:32.) In this final chapter, I want to answer some of the questions you may have about this form of prayer.

What is meditative prayer? How does it relate to meditation?

My description of meditative prayer is simple: with the help of the Holy Spirit, picture a godly truth and think about it over and over. In *The Purpose Driven Life*, Rick Warren defines meditation this way: "Meditation is *focused* thinking. It takes serious effort. You select a verse and reflect on it over and over in your mind. . . . If you know how to worry, you already know how to meditate."[18]

Although many Christians today shy away from the word *meditation* because of its New Age associations, meditation actually was a Christian practice long before the New Age movement came into being. And many Christian leaders today encourage Christian meditation because of the many benefits it brings:

Pastor Warren goes on to say: "No other habit can do more to transform your life and make you more like Jesus than daily reflection on Scripture. . . . If you look up all the times God speaks about meditation in the Bible, you will be amazed at the benefits he has promised to those who take the time to reflect on his Word throughout the day."[19]

Dr. Bruce Demarest, a professor of spiritual formation at Denver Seminary, writes: "A quieted heart is our best preparation for all this work of God. . . . Meditation refocuses us from ourselves and from the world so that we reflect on God's Word, His nature, His abilities, and His works. . . . So we prayerfully ponder, muse, and 'chew' the words of Scripture. . . . The goal is simply to permit the Holy Spirit to activate the life-giving Word of God."[20]

David, the "man after God's own heart," speaks often of meditating on God, his character, and his acts. God wants us to meditate—prayerfully reflect—on his Word day and night so that we will learn the truth and be able to obey it. The psalmist says that his delight is in the law of the Lord and in his law he meditates day and night (see Psalm 1:2). In the Old Testament, there are two primary Hebrew words for meditation: *hagah*, which means "to utter, groan, meditate, or ponder"; and *siyach*, which means "to muse, rehearse in one's mind, or contemplate." These words can also be translated as "to dwell on, to diligently consider, to heed."

With these definitions in mind, what do you most often "meditate" about? What is most often on your mind? Is it the truths of God? Or is it the concerns of your day, or something someone has said or done to you, recently or in the past? The truth is, everybody meditates at some point during the day.

What do you mean, "everybody meditates"?

Several years ago the Ketchum Global Research Network asked one thousand US adults between the ages of twenty-five and fifty-four what they typically think about as they shower. Their top four responses[21] were:

- To-do lists
- Problems and worries
- Daydreams
- Work

This offers an interesting look into what occupies our minds when we first get up in the morning or wind down in the evening, the two times when most of us take a shower. PreachingToday.com notes the irony:

> While we clean ourselves to start the day, we sully ourselves with stress and disappointment. When we try our best to clear the clutter from our minds with a nice long shower or bath in the evening, we fill our minds to overflowing with thoughts about places to go, people to see, dreams to fulfill.[22]

What would happen instead if we became people who filled our minds with God's Word, if we used the time when we cleaned our bodies to also cleanse our minds and spirits with God's truth about our lives, our relationships, our worries and cares?

Interestingly, the years when my health started going downhill coincided with a period when I began thinking over and over about what would happen if my husband died. And when did these fears haunt me most? As I was getting ready for the day each morning.

I distinctly remember these obsessive thoughts racing through my mind as I spent about twenty minutes blow-drying my hair in the morning. I tried fighting those negative thoughts but couldn't seem to help but picture the funeral and my life after his death, to the point that I would even cry while drying my hair.

All the pictures in my mind were of me failing to function well after his death, especially when I felt responsible for the church that we had founded together and helped build throughout the years. During that period, I was frequently meditating on the Perfect Lies, all the while thinking that I was simply trying to prepare myself for any possible catastrophe in the future! (By the way, Mark was in perfect health.)

Why is meditative prayer important?

Speaking on the topic of how we should think about prayer, Eugene Peterson speaks eloquently about the value of meditative prayer:

> Two commands direct us from the small-minded world of self-help to the large world of God's help. First, "Come, behold the works of the Lord." Take a long, scrutinizing look at what God is doing. This requires patient attentiveness and energetic concentration. Everyone else is noisier than God. The headlines and neon lights and amplifying systems of the world announce human works. But what of God's works? They are unadvertised but also inescapable, if we simply look. They are everywhere. They are marvelous. But God has no public relations

agency. He mounts no publicity campaign to get our attention. He simply invites us to look. . . .

The second command is, "Be still, and know that I am God." Be still. Quit rushing through the streets long enough to become aware that there is more to life than your little self-help enterprises. When we are noisy and when we are hurried, we are incapable of intimacy—deep, complex, personal relationships. If God is the living center of redemption, it is essential that we be in touch with and responsive to that personal will. If God has a will for this world and we want to be in on it, we must be still long enough to find out what it is. Baron von Hugel, who had a wise word on most subjects, always held out that "nothing was ever accomplished in a stampede."[23]

Christian meditation is always rooted in Scripture. In fact, the writers of the Bible tell us to meditate on its words: "Study this Book of Instruction continually. Meditate on it day and night so you will be sure to obey everything written in it. Only then will you prosper and succeed in all you do" (Joshua 1:8).

Why is meditative prayer so effective at demolishing Perfect Lies?

Consider David's words in Psalm 119:97-99:

Oh, how I love Your law!
It is my meditation all the day.

You, through Your commandments, make me wiser
than my enemies;
For they are ever with me.
I have more understanding than all my teachers,
For Your testimonies are my meditation. (NKJV)

"My enemies," who were "ever with me," were the Perfect Lies that had infiltrated the very programming of my subconscious mind. I didn't realize it, but I was accepting them as my reality. They were ever with me, and I didn't even recognize it.

Through meditative prayer, which enabled me to shine the light of truth on those Perfect Lies, I was able to expose and break the power of the faulty thought patterns I had lived with for years. That should come as no surprise, considering this promise from God's Word: "You will keep in perfect peace all who trust in you, all whose thoughts are fixed on you!" (Isaiah 26:3).

Our thoughts will ultimately determine our behavior, so what we think about is very important. That is why God wants us to think about his Word and meditate on his truth.

What role does God play in meditative prayer?

With God's involvement, there is an opportunity for my thoughts to join and align with the thoughts of the Creator of the universe; the Creator of all we see and know.

I have asked God to forgive me for my sins, and I have received the forgiveness that allows me to have a personal relationship with him and to continue living in his presence for all of eternity. The Holy Spirit, the Spirit of truth, is my counselor. Jesus told his disciples in John 15:26: "When the Counselor comes, whom I will send to you from the Father, the Spirit of truth who goes out from the Father, he will testify about me" (NIV). In John 16:13, he added: "When he, the Spirit of truth, comes, he will guide you into all truth. He will not speak on his own; he will speak only what he hears, and he will tell you what is yet to come" (NIV).

There is no doubt in my mind that my ability to discern the truth, identify the pictures that represented Perfect Lies, and then form true pictures came through the help of the Holy Spirit, who is the ultimate Counselor.

If you have never accepted Christ's forgiveness and placed your life under his authority, you can do that right now by praying this sincerely to God:

> Heavenly Father, I believe that Jesus Christ is your Son, the Son of God. Thank you for his dying on the cross for my sins. Please forgive my sins and give me the gift of eternal life. I ask Jesus into my life and heart to be my Lord and Savior. I want to serve you always. Your Word says if I will ask, I will receive the Holy Spirit. So in the name of Jesus Christ, my Lord, I am asking you to fill me to overflowing with your precious Holy Spirit. Thank you, Lord. I believe the Holy Spirit is within me, and by faith, I accept him and all of his guidance and power. Amen.

As the Holy Spirit helps heal your thoughts, you will notice that still, small voice of comfort and truth will become more prevalent than the Perfect Lies that have infiltrated your mind!

Are there any dangers or traps to be aware of as I begin meditative prayer?

I cannot think of any reason that should prevent you from beginning to try to communicate with God through meditative prayer. Some people feel intimidated or afraid about talking to God or communicating with him in any way because they are worried about "doing it wrong." That concern is understandable, since God is all-knowing and so much more powerful than we are. But let me assure you that he is more than willing to accept any attempt that you make to connect with him. Just as we would never forbid a child from interacting with a parent until he or she could speak in complete sentences, God will never turn away or reprimand your attempt to begin meditative prayer.

Jesus explained that our heavenly Father will willingly give the Holy Spirit, who is our Counselor, to anyone who asks:

> You fathers—if your children ask for a fish, do you give them a snake instead? Or if they ask for an egg, do you give them a scorpion? Of course not! So if you sinful people know how to give good gifts to your children, how much more will your heavenly

Father give the Holy Spirit to those who ask him. (Luke 11:11-13)

God does not expect us to be experts at communicating with him. He will lead you and guide you in all truth.

What should I expect when I begin meditative prayer?

If this type of prayer is new to you, you might find it difficult to let your mind be still. Don't worry if this happens; just keep returning your focus to God and appreciate the peace he is beginning to bring into your life.

You might experience strong emotions that surprise you. Do not suppress these. Release them to God and allow his healing Holy Spirit to flow through you and begin to touch those wounded and hurting places in your spirit. Such an emotional release can often bring relief, self-understanding, a greater revelation of God's love, growing intimacy with him, and even a physical response like crying or laughing, as your body begins to absorb the rest and peace that come.

You may hear God's still, small voice begin to speak to you. It may come as interiorly audible words, images, or pictures (visions), or it may come through dreams as you sleep. These do not have to be a part of your experience in order for God's healing to be made real in your life, but they do happen.

As you continue to meditate on God's truth, you will begin to experience a greater sense of God's presence bringing you some freeing new enlightenment, some new discovery on how to pray, or some new way to view your situation or what has happened to you in the past. His love will begin to permeate your spirit, healing all the broken places and filling you with joy, peace, and love.

Be prepared to be surprised and delighted. Jesus is our risen Savior who is alive and working through you. He is fully able to meet you at your point of need—and he longs to! He says to you, "Be sure of this: I am with you always" (Matthew 28:20).

How long should I spend in meditative prayer each day?

Five to seven minutes, three to five times per day, is ideal. Depending on the severity of the issues you are dealing with and how quickly you want to work through them, you may wish to devote more time to meditation each day. In general, the more focused time you spend, the quicker you will be able to reprogram your mind.

On one occasion, about six months after experiencing healing, I prayed for forty-five minutes for two or three days in a row, but that was a rare exception for me. I was preparing for a weeklong speaking engagement and was experiencing some anxiety and nervousness. As a result, I took some extra time to combat the Perfect Lies I was tempted to believe.

What if I don't have time to meditate?

When my counselor first told me to find three times during the day when I could sit quietly for five minutes, that practice seemed so foreign to me that I could hardly imagine it.

To this day, I am pretty sure that had I not been desperate and at the end of my rope, I would not have attempted the seemingly miraculous feat of stopping for five minutes three times per day. But since I was sick and in my bathrobe most of the day, I had plenty of time.

I had decided to take a three-month sabbatical from my work at the church, but I was still trying to run the busy household of a megachurch pastor and care for our five active children, who were between the ages of seventeen and four. Even though people in the church were bringing food for our family every day for about two months, I continued to be driven by an inner slave master who told me that my only value was to work, work, work!

I had lived my whole life thinking that if I had any energy in my body, it was for the purpose of work. Rest and reflection were only a necessary evil until you could get back to *work*! I didn't know it at the time, but I have since learned that if I don't have some creative, intuitive thinking time (and it does take time), you might as well ask me to go without water or food.

Since I had been in "mommy boot camp" for so many years with my body, mind, and soul taxed to the limit, I was completely numb to my own needs. I was in a very destructive pattern of driving myself mercilessly. I was everyone else's mother, but I needed a mother to tell me to go to bed, to eat a snack, to go to recess, and to go to my room for a time-out!

Of course, when you make a child take a time-out, they generally scream and cry at first. When they rejoin the rest of the family, however, you are generally rewarded with a much more happy, humble, and focused child. This is exactly what meditative prayer does for me. It helps me take a "time-out" to adjust my attitude, focus, and take a pause, a breath, to love myself and say, *Everything's going to be all right, Jennifer. You're fine. Everything's fine.*

This practice allows me to put my problems and issues into perspective. When I look out my window to see the clouds, sky, grass, and trees, I realize that there is a bigger world out there that carries on in spite of the issues that seem to be towering in my mind. My issues are temporary, but the world does not seem to be affected by them—it's not coming to an end because of them!

When you make meditative prayer a priority, you will discover many times during the day when you can actively turn over God's Word in your mind. Just before you fall asleep is a great time; you can have God's Word be the last thing that occupies your mind. Then, upon awakening, you can have God's Word be the first thing to fill your mind as you start each day. I naturally wake up early, before anyone else in my house, and many times as I get out of bed, I just sit right down on the floor of the bedroom to spend five minutes in meditative prayer.

What about at other times during the day? The main requirements for meditative prayer are that you be alone and uninterrupted and able to sit or lie comfortably. Here are some possible times and places to find space to pray:

- Close the door to your office and take a meditative prayer break.
- Take a bath instead of a shower and use five minutes during the bath for meditative prayer.
- When in your car, if you have extra time to kill between appointments, pull over into a parking lot or deserted area. (I have designated places that I have used all over my city!)
- If your house is full of people and your husband is in the bedroom, go to a walk-in closet if you have one and sit on the floor to pray.
- Tell your children, "Mommy is going to go to her room for five minutes to pray. If an emergency comes up, I will be right there, but if not, let Mommy take some quiet time alone with God."
- Moms, you can even allow or encourage your very young babies or toddlers to be a part of your meditation time. They can sit quietly with you and, depending on their age, repeat Scripture after you. Pretty soon, however, they usually get bored and move on to something else while you try to keep your focus!
- Excuse yourself to go to the restroom, but use that time for meditative prayer instead.
- Use the bathroom stall of an airport.
- If you can't get alone while riding in an airplane or a car with others, pretend you are asleep but actually be silently practicing meditative prayer.
- Take a break outdoors on the patio or balcony.

Can meditative prayer help me on those nights when I can't sleep?

Yes, in fact David seemed to rely on it during the nights he couldn't rest, perhaps because of the enemies like Saul who were trying to hunt him down. While hiding out in the wilderness of Judah, David cried out to God:

> When I remember You on my bed,
> I meditate on You in the night watches.
> Because You have been my help,
> Therefore in the shadow of Your wings I will rejoice.
> My soul follows close behind You;
> Your right hand upholds me. (Psalm 63:6-8, NKJV)

Often we feel most alone at night, when the hours stretch before us and we are alone with our thoughts and fears. At such times, I find comfort from the following psalm because it describes so well what was happening with me for all those months when I could not sleep more than five hours at a time in the night.

> I call to remembrance my song in the night;
> I meditate within my heart,
> And my spirit makes diligent search. (Psalm 77:6, NKJV)

During the lonely times in the middle of the night, I often sat by myself in my bathroom and looked out the window to see the full moon shining still and quiet, spreading its silvery glow over all the room. On one of these nights, I was reminded of the children's rhyme:

I see the moon.
The moon sees me.
God bless the moon,
And God bless me.

As I stared at that beautiful moon, I was still coming out of the fog of lies that had me bound. It dawned on me that the truth was that *God sees me*. I had a simple but profound revelation of his love. The tears began to flow as I looked up at that moon. Everyone else in the house (and in the whole world, it seemed) was sound asleep, but God was awake and he loved me. I realized that I would always have a special memory—a beautiful truthful picture in my collection—and every time I saw God's amazing moon, I would remember that he loves me. Out of that experience came the words to this song:

The heavens tell the story of your love.
Ever I will lift my eyes above.
Wash me with your rain upon my face.
Kiss me with your gentle winds of grace.
Fill me with light from heaven's sky.
Let the sun kiss every sorrow dry.
I see the moon.

You see me.
I see the stars.
You shine in me.
Clouds flow by.
You'll never leave.
Your love is unchanging.
Your love changes me.[24]

How long did you engage in meditative prayer before you were confident you had overcome all the Perfect Lies in your mind?

It took me about three years of actively, purposefully meditating to truly change my thoughts. Yes, I said *years*. However, I saw initial, radical results in as little as six weeks.

What makes up meditative prayer?

There are four components of the type of meditative prayer that I practice, which broke the power of the lying thoughts in my mind and heart and healed my body, mind, and soul. I believe that all four of these components were essential for me to reprogram, or as the Bible says, "renew" my mind in order for my body to be healed. What I am describing here is nothing new. It is as old as the Bible; it is essentially basic, simple, mind-transforming prayer, but descriptively broken down into components that might be more understandable to some who have never thought of it this way before. These four components are:

1. Knowing the truth
2. Identifying the lie
3. Forming the true picture
4. Physically sitting and meditating

Knowing the truth

Knowing the truth about God is as easy as picking up an understandable version of the Bible and reading it. The more you read it, the more you will know it. If you don't like to read, you can pick up a set of CDs at almost any bookstore and enjoy the Bible being read aloud to you in your home or car.

Knowing the truth is as simple as being a part of a life-giving church where God's truth is taught to you on a regular basis. Knowing the truth is as simple as reading books such as this one, in which I demonstrate how God's truth is the antidote to the Perfect Lies that have infiltrated your thinking. Knowing the truth is a lifelong pursuit that should never end.

Fortunately, years of living the Christian faith had prepared me with the knowledge of the truth that I needed to receive healing in my body and soul. Jesus said that you will know the truth and the truth will set you free (see John 8:32). I knew the truth on a certain level as data in my brain, but I didn't really *know*, comprehend, and fully understand with an ability to apply the truth. For me, it wasn't so much a matter of adding more data—it was a matter of finding a systematic approach that would correct my programming bit by bit (or neuropathway by neuropathway). The Bible refers to the renewing of the mind as the washing with water of the Word (see Ephesians 5:26). After the old programming is exposed as faulty, it is wiped out and the new programming is implemented through repeated meditative prayer.

Identifying the lie

Much of this book was written to help us identify the Perfect Lies that have become so ingrained into the fabric of our thinking that we accept them as truth. We are conditioned or programmed to accept ways of thinking based on our past experiences. One result is what psychologists call "learned helplessness." As a result of undergoing repeated unpleasant or harmful circumstances, both people and animals continue to behave helplessly, even when they're given the opportunity to avoid that negative situation. Not surprisingly, this often leads to passivity and depression.

If you've ever seen a circus elephant, you may have seen a living example of learned helplessness. Pastor David Dykes notes that these animals are often tied to a small wooden stake, and a grown elephant could easily pull it out of the ground and go free. However, when handlers train baby elephants, they shackle the animals to a strong iron anchor bar that they drive deep into the ground. When the little elephants try to get away, they cannot. They also feel pain from the pull of the shackle on their legs. Eventually the elephants give up and stop pulling. Dykes says:

As the elephant grows up, they replace the iron anchor bar with a wooden stake. That's why the grown elephant doesn't pull away; he doesn't think he can, so he can't. It's not the stake in the ground keeping him in place; it's the thought in his mind that keeps him there.[25]

In order to accept the truth of God for your life, you must identify the lies that have falsely imprisoned you, just as that wooden stake needlessly kept the elephant captive. It is also important to remember that a lie in your mind will usually take shape as a false picture or image. So in order to identify the lie, it is helpful to start with the picture or image you have in your mind. Here are some examples:

- A picture or memory of a teacher punishing you might be contributing to the lie, I must be perfect because my actions define who I am.
- An image or memory of a particular conversation with a well-dressed, wealthy person might be contributing to the lie, I must indulge myself in order to be happy.
- An image of abuse might be contributing to the lie, I must always be on guard because trouble is all around me.
- An image of a conversation with your former spouse might be contributing to the lie, I must meet the standards others have set for me because otherwise I will be unlovable.

To identify which of the nine Perfect Lies you believe, try to identify a picture of a recent event or memory that is bothering you. Keep in mind that pictures are just as real to us as actual events, even if they never physically happened. So a lying picture could be just as powerful even if it were the figment of your imagination. Do not overlook pictures or even dreams that are imaginary.

When trying to identify the lie as you meditate, carefully examine the picture in your mind for flaws or fallacies. Use the Scriptures and references in this book to help you determine what part of that picture is a lie. Some pictures are trickier to decipher than others. Ask the Holy Spirit to help by shining his light of truth on the picture in your mind.

Sometimes it is hard for me to identify exactly with which lie I may be struggling because I am dealing with more than one at the same time. Perhaps I am reflecting on a picture that helps but something about the situation is still bothering me. That's okay. The process that I describe here is simple, but it's not always easy. I can usually tell when a truthful picture I've formed is effective because I generally experience a feeling of relief, joy, or a release of emotion as that new picture develops.

Occasionally, it may take you several sessions of meditative prayer to determine the Perfect Lie that has deceived you. You can always pick up your examination of that mental image the next time you engage in meditative prayer. If this happens, just thank God that he is in the process of renewing your mind. It can also be helpful to ask a trusted friend who has godly insight or a counselor to help you impartially view a situation and find the truth, especially if you are consistently having a hard time identifying the Perfect Lie in a certain image.

Forming the true picture

As I've mentioned many times, most human thoughts are stored in the form of pictures. I believe that is one reason Jesus used parables to illustrate spiritual truths. He knew that once people formed a picture in their minds, they would believe what they "saw."

Experts in memory use this method as well. Perhaps you've heard of the systems that help people memorize names or facts and figures by associating those things with a specific picture.

Here's an illustration of how this works: If a person is driving down the highway listening to the radio and hears a traffic report about a four-car accident several miles ahead of him, his mind immediately begins forming a picture to fit the description of what he is hearing. Depending on the various thoughts and filters already programmed into his brain and depending on the picture he forms in his mind, he will actually begin to have physiological responses to the pictures he is "seeing." His blood pressure may begin to rise, his heart rate may elevate, and he may begin to perspire, all because he is picturing any number of situations—from his being late to an appointment because of the traffic delay to his fear that a friend or loved one might be involved in the accident.

What has changed in this man's environment from one mile to the next? Nothing—*outside of his body*. His air conditioner is still on; his car speed is steady. He cannot physically see anything that would make him aware of a car accident, but because he heard something on the radio, the pictures in his mind have changed, causing his body to act as if he were actually experiencing the accident firsthand.

This is the power of pictures or thoughts. They can elicit a physiological response as authentic as any real-life situation. What if those pictures in our minds are based on lies, deception, or untruths?

On a deeper level, what if the pictures that have been stored in *your mind* since childhood are based on untruths or lies that you have accepted as true? Perhaps they are so familiar to you that *you don't even realize they are there*, much less realize they are lies.

This is why, when I engage in meditative prayer, I purposefully identify and/or create a picture that represents the truth as I know it from Scripture. In order to do this, I have to allow my imagination to roam freely for a constructive purpose. I find that a good place to start is by trying to picture God or Jesus being physically present in an image. In fact, because I know that God is everywhere, that he is aware of everything that happens, and that he is always with us, this perception is true.

To find a picture of truth, I usually start by asking myself the following questions regarding the situation about which I am thinking:

- Where was God or Jesus in this situation/picture?
- What was God or Jesus doing in the situation/picture?
- What was his response to me as the events unfolded?
- What was his response to the others in the situation?

Sometimes it is hard work to visually "picture" the truth when you have so firmly believed a lie. That is why you must take time to sit and do nothing else. Sometimes it is hard to know what the truth of a certain situation actually is. Draw on the help of the Holy Spirit and Scripture to identify the truth. Don't be discouraged if things don't happen quickly or easily. Your brain didn't create the intricate programming that controls your life in just one day; that programming has developed over the course of every second of every day since the day of your birth.

The changes you are making as you form truthful pictures are instantaneous in your brain cells, but you may not see noticeable results in your physical body or emotions until those changes reach a critical mass. In her book *Who Switched Off My Brain?*, Caroline Leaf describes the neuron cells in our brains as looking like trees. The more developed a thought, the more branches there are on a tree. As a lie is scrutinized and contrasted with a new truth, the neural structure of the cells actually changes bit by bit as the branches on the false belief begin to wither and new neuropathways form. As the truth begins to overtake the lies, you will find at some point that the untruths begin crashing down and you will see everything much more clearly.

Physically sitting and meditating

For most of my life, I had no idea how much value there is in sitting quietly and purposely thinking about something over and over. Yet this was one of the most important factors that led to my being healed in body, mind, and spirit. Meditative prayer is the actual time spent renewing your mind. I was definitely engaging in meditation before I was healed, but it was time spent pondering lies that I thought were true. My mind would get into a rut, with my thoughts spinning around and around in a negative fashion. Usually this was subconscious, so I wasn't even aware of the destruction being done.

For some reason, I had thought that prayer consisted chiefly of my taking time to talk to God about my issues. I also quoted the Bible during prayer to confess the truth of the Word of God. At times I sensed God's Spirit "speaking" to me through my spirit, as the Bible says the Holy Spirit is our Counselor and brings things to our remembrance (see John 14:26). But I had no clue that I could or should meditate quietly for the purpose of changing my thoughts by changing the pictures in my heart and mind.

When you begin, put your hands and body in a physical position of prayer. This, I feel, is an extremely important part of meditative prayer. I wish I could say this doesn't matter, but my experience has been that what my hands and body are doing matters very much toward the effectiveness of my focus and concentration. When we meditate, we are connecting with God, whom we cannot experience through our five physical senses.

If you were taught to pray as a child, you learned to fold your hands and bow your head. Why? Was this just tradition? Was there some supernatural power activated because your hands were touching or because your eyes were closed or your head was bowed? I don't believe so; however, closing your eyes, bowing your head, and folding your hands help you focus. Also, as soon as you close your eyes, alpha waves begin to be activated in your brain, which are conducive to deep thinking.

Every time I practice meditative prayer, I put my hands in a position of prayer. Just as a small child learns to fold her hands when she prays, I have found that as an adult, I need help in focusing my mind, body, soul, and faith during my prayers.

I have found it helpful to have physical points of contact as I engage in meditative prayer to help me concentrate and stay on task.

Here are some of the physical positions I recommend:

- *Sit up straight.* I have found that sitting straight is more effective than just carelessly slouching over or leaning. I mostly sit with legs crossed on the floor, but at times I will sit on a bench or chair or in the seat of a car if I take a meditation break in the car. (Of course, I am not driving at the same time!) This position says to my body, "I mean business. It is time for prayer. Get focused."

- *Lie quietly.* Some of my favorite times of meditation take place while I'm lying in bed. This is great when you are awakened in the middle of the night or if you just want to take a break anytime. I lie flat on my back with my hands across my chest and my fingertips together.

- *Breathe deeply, slowly, and calmly.* This slow, relaxed breathing helps you to let go of the tension, to take your mind off of your problems and focus.

- *Put your hands in a position of prayer.* Some of the positions I have used during my prayer times include fingertips together, palms together, hands upraised, palms facing upward in my lap, fingertips on my temples, hands on a body part that needs healing, fingertips on my throat or thyroid gland, hand on my forehead, hand on the back of my neck.

- *Speak out loud.* I verbally intersperse confessions, positive statements, or Scripture. I repeat a focus statement or Scripture every thirty seconds to a minute or so. When I first learned meditative prayer, I found I could not meditate in silence; I needed to engage my speaking and hearing to help my mind concentrate. I have included some statements and Scriptures at the end of each chapter, which you may find very effective as you speak them out loud during meditative prayer.

- *Visualize with your mind.* This is the concrete way to form new pictures associated with truth, which will in essence reprogram your thoughts. Do it. It works.

Once my body is in position, I usually start by asking God to fill me with his light, life, and love. I always thank him for doing this from the very beginning of my meditation session. I say: *Thank you, Lord, for filling me with the light, life, and love of Jesus Christ. I thank you, Lord, that Jesus' light, life, and love are flowing through every cell of my body and every fiber of my being. I thank you, God, that every dark place in my mind or body is being illuminated by the light, life, and love of Jesus Christ.*

Then I usually pick from a few different focus options. If something is troubling me or I am battling stress or physical symptoms, I take the Lie Detector Test:

- I ask myself, *What am I feeling right now?* I try to identify the actual emotion I am feeling, whether it be sadness, fear, discouragement, abandonment, or frustration. I try to give it a descriptive word, which I say out loud.
- I then ask myself, *When is the first time I remember feeling that emotion?* I have found that my emotions have thought patterns associated with pictures. It seems that the first picture that is ingrained in my mind usually holds the power to all the other pictures of similar situations that have happened afterward.

If I can shatter the original picture, then the others begin to deteriorate as well. For example, if you are feeling lonely or alone and it is making you sad, then after you have identified that emotion of loneliness, ask yourself when you can first remember feeling that way. Go back through all the pictures in your mind to the very beginning to the first time you ever felt alone. What was happening? What is the picture you see? When I identify the picture of that first time, I try to analyze the picture, not from my point of view at the time it happened, but from my "grown-up" point of view—as impartially as possible.

- Then I ask myself, *What lie did I believe?* I try to identify which of the Perfect Lies I am tempted to believe. I go through the list, if necessary, to discern the truth.

- I then ask myself, *What is the genuine truth in this picture? What is the antidote?* As I think about the reality of what was truthfully happening, I experiment with changing my memory of the picture to reflect my newly realized truth. Sometimes, I have to "try out" several different options until I find the picture that effectively brings a feeling of joy or relief.

As I form the truthful picture and meditate on it, I have noticed that I usually experience a physical indication of stress relief. Frequently, I will begin to smile, or laugh, or tears will come to my eyes. Early on, when the lies were so ingrained in my thinking and my situation was so desperate, I would sometimes sob almost uncontrollably as a powerful picture of God's love came into focus. I believe this was a cleansing of my soul and a physical release as the Perfect Lies were exposed and their power was obliterated. There is something very real and very spiritual that can happen when you first experience the revelation of a lie and the ensuing truth as it reverberates through your soul. It reminds me of the scene in *The Wizard of Oz* when Glinda the Good Witch tells the Wicked Witch so matter-of-factly: "Be gone! You have no power here!" When those Perfect Lies are exposed, they have no more power to control your thoughts or actions.

What are some ideas for meditation if there is nothing in particular troubling me?

If all is well in my life and nothing particularly is bothering me, I might choose to:

- Reflect on a previous picture on which I have been focusing recently (i.e., from my previous session).
- Select a good, truthful picture from the past—one of my favorites—and meditate on it, replaying it over and over in my mind.
- Select a Scripture that I have memorized and recite it. As I do, I go slowly and stop as necessary to form or develop new, meaningful pictures to go with the words of the passage.
- Select a song that is meaningful to me. I either sing

the song or recite the words. As I do, I make up my own original music video complete with hair blowing in the wind as Jesus and I dance together. I've even pictured Jesus playing electric guitar, mandolin, or violin. I know this sounds silly, but there is nothing wrong with picturing Jesus with me in any scenario. Since I am a musician, it helps me to personify his love for me. You could picture Jesus involved in any activity you enjoy, such as sports, camping, cooking, etc.

· Engage in meditative prayer while listening to a musical recording. When I do this, I picture the lyrics as they apply to God and me, or Jesus and me.

How should I end my time of meditative prayer?

I close each session by thanking God for loving me so much that he has shown me his truth. I thank him for healing me and setting me free. I thank him that I no longer walk in the darkness of lies, but that I am free to walk in the light of his truth. I stand up refreshed, free of stress, and ready for the rest of my life.

Acknowledgments

I WANT TO acknowledge and thank Jan Long Harris and the team at Tyndale House for believing in the story of God's healing in my life. I especially want to thank my editor, Kim Miller, who helped turn these thoughts into principles and who encouraged me to bring more stories to light. Kim, in my eyes you are a genius. You made this process a joy, and I always looked forward to every e-mail and conversation with you. Thanks for making my first experience with writing a book an enjoyable one. I also want to thank:

- Maggie Payne, for the hours of transcribing, proofing, and writing the first draft of the workbook, and for all of her helpful feedback, done with excellence and a cheerful attitude.
- Jake Jones, for first believing in the idea for a book and encouraging me to write it.
- the people of Victory Church and my many friends for allowing me to write this book in front of them as they

watched me live it out and heard me tell my stories publicly.

- the staff at Victory Church, especially Victory Productions, for helping put wings to my dream and creating a visual/ artistic environment for this message to flourish effectively at church and through multimedia.
- Alex Loyd and the people in his organization who were there when I cried out to God for help and healing and pointed me on my journey.
- my mom and dad for providing a stable and loving environment that enabled me to easily accept the love of my heavenly Father. Thanks for always believing in me.
- my daughter Victoria, who has grown into a young lady. During my deepest struggles, she was a toddler and one of my meditative prayer companions. She now cheerfully endures my geekiness and embarrassing moments in our cherished times together.
- my son Joseph who, as the fourth child, could easily have felt forgotten or neglected as his mom was struggling through her own issues, but who always faces life with humor, innovation, creativity, and confidence. Thanks for telling me to lighten up and making me laugh.
- my son Andrew for his care, concern, stability, and support—always honest, but affectionate and kind. I love having you in my life and knowing I can count on you through hard times and easy times, good times and bad times.
- my daughter Evangelyn for helping me see the world in a

different way. Sensitive, compassionate to the underdog, and willing to see hurting people from a different perspective, you helped me look outside my preconceived ideas to learn how to help others more effectively.

- my son Chris for believing in the power of this message. You played an integral part in refining the nine Perfect Lies. Thanks for offering your insight into human nature and the hours of study of personality types, which helped to formulate the final versions of the Lies. Thank for loving me and being willing to listen nonjudgmentally to my sometimes-crazy ideas.

- My husband, Mark, who has not only passionately loved me for thirty years but who has provided a protective support system in which I and our children have flourished. He was the first one to hear about the Perfect Lies as he was there each day experiencing them with me firsthand. He was also the first one to rejoice with me as each day I would share with him as a new lie was being exposed. The power of his steadfast belief in me and his funding of all my "projects" cannot be underestimated. Thanks so much for your patience, perseverance, and belief, not only in our marriage, but in the gifts God has put in me.

Discussion Guide

CHAPTER 1—PERFECT LIES IN ACTION

1. Jennifer attempted to overcome her physical ailments with the help of doctors, medications, and even diets. Why do you think she couldn't find relief?

2. While you may never have experienced the extreme health problems that Jennifer did, can you tell of a time when your emotional state negatively impacted your life in some way? As you look back at that time, can you identify any lying thoughts that may have exacerbated the problem?

3. Why do you think Jennifer refers to the destructive untruths we subconsciously tell ourselves as "Perfect Lies"?

4. Jennifer introduces meditative prayer with an illustration of how she pictured the Father, Son, and

Holy Spirit comforting her in her living room. If you were to imagine God loving you unconditionally, what would that picture look like?

CHAPTER 2—PICTURES ARE POWERFUL!

1. Jennifer writes that as your brain takes in information through your five senses, "you translate those details (either consciously or subconsciously) into mental pictures. When you think a thought, you generally are not reading that thought like the words on a page scrolling through the screen of your mind. You are reading that thought by seeing it in pictures in your mind's eye." To test her assertion, think about a powerful memory. What comes to mind?

2. The basic human emotions are happiness, sadness, fear, anger, disgust, and surprise. Explain what you think Jennifer means when she refers to them as the six "emotional senses."

3. "People get into trouble when they either suppress their emotions or when their emotions, which are intended to be temporary, smolder for too long" (page 30). Do you tend to suppress your emotions or let them smolder? Can you recall a time when that led you into difficulty?

4. In 2 Corinthians 10:4, the apostle Paul talks of "strongholds" created in our minds. Do you agree

with Jennifer that these might include recurring false thoughts that dominate your thinking? Could you give an example of such a lie?

CHAPTER 3—WHAT IS THE TRUTH?

1. Scripture calls Satan the father of lies. What can you learn from Genesis 3:1-7 about his techniques for deceiving you and other people?

2. What else do we learn about the Accuser from John 8:44 and John 10:10?

3. What is the most potent weapon you have to defend yourself from Satan's lies?

4. What are some ways you might allow God's Word to combat the lies in your own mind?

CHAPTER 4—PERFECT LIE NUMBER ONE: I AM UNLOVABLE

1. Have you ever battled the Perfect Lie: "I must meet the standards others have set for me because otherwise I will be unlovable"? If so, can you give an example of how this affected you?

2. What kinds of things do you tend to say to yourself when you make a mistake? Are you affirmative or disapproving with yourself? What does that tell you about your susceptibility to this Perfect Lie?

3. On page 59, Jennifer writes, "The lie that we are lovable only if we meet others' expectations is a distortion of the truth, with just enough veracity thrown in to make it seem believable." Is this true in your own life? If so, give an example.

4. Why do you think Jennifer found it wasn't enough simply to read a few passages from the Bible to counteract the lie that she was unlovable? How does she recommend you interact with God's Word when trying to counteract a Perfect Lie?

CHAPTER 5—PERFECT LIE NUMBER TWO: I AM WORTHLESS

1. Have you ever battled the Perfect Lie: "I must prove myself because my worth depends on what I do"? If so, can you give an example of how this affected you?

2. If you struggle with this lie, you may (1) conclude that God doesn't know what he is doing when he calls you to do things for him; (2) look back at all your failures and wonder whether God can really use you; (3) be easily discouraged by others' criticism; or (4) feel hurt by a sharp word or a disapproving look directed at you. Which of these four reactions do you identify with most?

3. If you identify with the feelings of worthlessness and hopelessness described in this chapter, take a few moments today to ask yourself, *When is the first time I can remember experiencing this emotion?* Once you

unearth a picture in your mind of that experience, see if you can apply the truth of one of the Statements or Scriptures to Ponder on pages 91–94 to that situation.

4. "Worth is measured by how much value is placed on a person or object by the one who loves it" (page 88). Read Psalm 23. What phrase speaks to you most powerfully of your worth and value to God?

CHAPTER 6—PERFECT LIE NUMBER THREE: I AM UNACCEPTABLE

1. Have you ever battled the Perfect Lie: "I must gain the acceptance of others because their opinion matters most"? If so, can you give an example of how this affected you?

2. Throughout history, entire people groups have been sent the message that they're unacceptable. Can you name one example? How has that negatively affected that particular group? The people who oppressed that group?

3. If you buy into this lie for yourself, you may try to avoid conflict or appear outwardly perfect. How significant are these issues for you?

4. What did considering the story of Zacchaeus (see Luke 19:1-10) teach you about how God views you?

CHAPTER 7—PERFECT LIE NUMBER FOUR: I AM UNABLE

1. Have you ever battled the Perfect Lie: "I must pull back because I am less capable than others"? If so, can you give an example of how this affected you?

2. How might this lie have interfered with God's plan to use Jennifer to reach out to the people of Lesotho? Have you ever been tempted not to do something you felt God was calling you to do because of this lie?

3. Can you, like Jennifer, tell of a time when God demonstrated his strength in the midst of your weakness? If so, share your story.

4. Romans 8:11 tells Christ-followers that "the Spirit of God, who raised Jesus from the dead, lives in you." Do you live as if this is true? Explain.

CHAPTER 8—PERFECT LIE NUMBER FIVE: I AM A TARGET

1. Have you ever battled the Perfect Lie: "I must protect myself because others are out to get me"? If so, can you give an example of how this affected you?

2. Have you ever known someone like Aunt Lucille? If so, what effect did that person have on those around him or her?

3. Why does believing this lie make it particularly difficult for someone to draw close to God and other people?

4. When we're in self-protective mode, do you agree that it can be helpful to try to picture the situation from the other person's perspective? Why or why not?

CHAPTER 9—PERFECT LIE NUMBER SIX: I AM NOT ANGRY

1. Have you ever battled the Perfect Lie: "I must avoid conflict because expressing my anger is wrong"? If so, can you give an example of how this affected you?

2. Why are those who give in to this lie so vulnerable to manipulation?

3. Read Matthew 10:14 and John 2:13-17. What do these passages teach us about what disturbs Jesus and how we should express anger?

4. Would you say you generally express or suppress your anger? What can Ephesians 4:26-27 teach you about how to handle this emotion?

CHAPTER 10—PERFECT LIE NUMBER SEVEN: I AM BAD

1. Have you ever battled the Perfect Lie: "I must be perfect because my actions define who I am"? If so, can you give an example of how this affected you?

2. Jennifer says, "Our biggest mistake when dealing with this guilt is trying to handle it on our own" (page 177). If you struggle with feelings that you are bad, how do you try to deal with that pain?

3. If you believe this untruth, you may have difficulty seeing the difference between *you* and *your behavior*. How do Scripture passages like Psalm 103:8-14, Romans 3:21-26, and 1 John 1:9 help you see that distinction?

4. Do you have one or more pictures in your mind that seem to confirm the lie that you are guilty and not worthy of love? If so, take some time to pray, *Holy Spirit, please show me a picture of the truth that was happening in that situation.* After dwelling on this for a few minutes, read the Statements and Scriptures to Ponder on page 190 and ask him to show you the antidote to the lie you have believed. If you are discussing these questions with a group, consider sharing your experience with others.

CHAPTER 11—PERFECT LIE NUMBER EIGHT: I AM IN DANGER

1. Have you ever battled the Perfect Lie: "I must always be on guard because trouble is all around me"? If so, can you give an example of how this affected you?

2. For much of her life, Jennifer was consumed by the fear that she would be emotionally abandoned by those closest to her. How would you describe your greatest fear?

3. What do you think distinguishes healthy fear from unhealthy fear?

4. Take a few minutes to think of yourself in the midst of the situation that causes you the most fear. Now imagine Jesus right there with you. How does that change your perception of the situation you fear most?

CHAPTER 12—PERFECT LIE NUMBER NINE: I AM DEPRIVED

1. Have you ever battled the Perfect Lie: "I must indulge myself in order to be happy"? If so, can you give an example of how this affected you?

2. Joe Stowell calls our dissatisfaction "the Eve factor" (see page 215). What exactly do you think he means by that? What evidence do you see of it at work in our world today?

3. Does your heart more often reflect the attitude "I have learned to feel deprived in every situation" or "I have learned to be content in every situation"? Explain.

4. How do the emotions associated with this Perfect Lie— impatience, anger, frustration, insecurity, and craving for love substitutes (addictions)—get in the way of the contentment we can find in Christ?

CHAPTER 13—QUESTIONS AND ANSWERS ABOUT CHRISTIAN MEDITATIVE PRAYER

1. What do you think of Jennifer's statement that we all meditate on something (see page 233)? What have you

learned from this book about how to meditate in a productive and God-honoring way?

2. Why are God's Word and the Holy Spirit so integral to meditative prayer?

3. The idea of finding time to spend in meditative prayer may seem daunting. After reviewing the suggestions on page 244, how might you find time to incorporate five minutes of meditative prayer into your schedule a few times each day?

4. As you worked through this book, what Perfect Lie did you identify as the one distorting your thinking and well-being the most? What steps have you taken (or do you now plan to take) to counteract that lie?

Notes

1. Chris is now a producer, songwriter, and performer who started the group Warr Acres. Their first album reached number seven on the Christian iTunes chart.
2. Caroline Leaf, *Who Switched Off My Brain?* (Nashville: Thomas Nelson, 2009).
3. Jennifer and Chris Crow, "Redeemed," Victory Productions, 2007.
4. Sharon Cohen, "Faces beyond the Numbers of Long-Term Unemployed," Associated Press, February 11, 2012.
5. Quote from Kim Cameron, an organizational psychologist with the University of Michigan, in Louis Uchitelle, *The Disposable American: Layoffs and Their Consequences* (New York: Knopf, 2006), 181.
6. Daniel Bates, "'I Want to Die': Chilling Letters of Boy, 13, 'Kept in Dog Cage and Beaten to Death by Parents,'" *DailyMailOnline*, June 27, 2011, http://www.dailymail.co.uk/news/article-2008765/Chilling-letters -Christian-Coate-boy-kept-dog-cage-parents.html. See also Ruth Ann Krause, "Dad, Stepmom Charged in Murder of Boy Found under Concrete Slab," *Chicago Sun-Times*, May 10, 2011, http://www.suntimes .com/news/metro/5294165-418/dad-stepmom-charged-with-murder-in -death-of-boy-found-under-concrete-slab-in-gary.html.
7. Kenneth S. Davis, "Miss Eleanor Roosevelt," *American Heritage* 22, no. 6 (October 1971), http://www.americanheritage.com/content/miss -eleanor-roosevelt.
8. A saying of unknown origin, quoted by Kirbyjon H. Caldwell, *Be In It to Win It* (New York: Touchstone Faith, 2007), 25, emphasis added.
9. Nick Vujicic, *Life without Limits* (New York: Doubleday, 2010), 1–2.

10. See Philippians 4:13.

11. Lee Strobel, "Meet the Jesus I Know," Tape 211 from www.Preaching TodaySermons.com, a ministry of Christianity Today.

12. The 1662 revision of the Prayer of Humble Access; see http://en.wikipedia .org/wiki/Prayer_of_Humble_Access.

13. See http://bible.org/illustration/average-person%e2%80%99s-anxiety -focused-on%e2%80%a6.

14. See http://www.sermonillustrations.com/a-z/w/worry.htm.

15. See Psalm 17:8 and Isaiah 49:16.

16. Joseph Stowell, *Jesus Nation* (Carol Stream, IL: Tyndale House, 2009), 131–132.

17. Carlin Flora, "The Pursuit of Happiness," *Psychology Today*, January 2009, http://www.psychologytoday.com/articles/200812/the-pursuit-happiness.

18. Rick Warren, *The Purpose Driven Life* (Grand Rapids, MI: Zondervan, 2001), 190.

19. Ibid.

20. Bruce Demarest, *Satisfy Your Soul* (Colorado Springs: NavPress, 1999), 133.

21. Anne Carey and Sam Ward, "Snapshots: What Do You Think About in the Shower?" *USA Today*, June 5, 2009, quoted by Van Morris and Brian Lowery, "What We're Thinking about as the Day Begins and Ends," PreachingToday.com, August 3, 2009, http://www.preachingtoday.com /illustrations/2009/august/5080309.html.

22. Ibid.

23. Eugene Peterson, "Thinking Correctly about Prayer," http://media .sermonaudio.com/mediapdf/419091952361.pdf.

24. Jennifer Crow and Chris Crow, "Heavens Tell," Victory Productions, 2005.

25. David Dykes, "When You Get Bent Out of Shape," sermon based on Luke 13:10-21, http://www.preaching.com/sermons/11578574/page-2/.

About the Author

JENNIFER CROW is passionate, intense, authentic, and committed to helping others live victoriously. She and her husband, Pastor Mark Crow, have served at Victory Church, a multisite congregation in Oklahoma, since founding it in 1994. Jennifer is a graduate of Oral Roberts University and founder of the Beautiful Dream Society, an organization dedicated to fighting human trafficking in Lesotho. She and Mark are the parents of five treasured children.

Fix your thoughts on what is true, and honorable, and right, and pure, and lovely, and admirable. Think about things that are excellent and worthy of praise. (Philippians 4:8)

277